G000055235

SONGS ANI

SONGS AND SERMONS

John Wesley and Charles Wesley

Introduction by Robert Van de Weyer

Fount
An Imprint of HarperCollins*Publishers*

Fount Paperbacks is an Imprint of
HarperCollins*Religious*
Part of HarperCollins*Publishers*
77–85 Fulham Palace Road, London W6 8JB

First published in Great Britain
in 1996 by Fount Paperbacks

1 3 5 7 9 10 8 6 4 2

Copyright in the Introduction © 1996
by Robert Van de Weyer

A catalogue record for this book is
available from the British Library

ISBN 0 00 628012 9

Printed and bound in Great Britain by
Caledonian International Book Manufacturing Ltd, Glasgow

CONDITIONS OF SALE

This book is sold subject to the condition that it
shall not, by way of trade or otherwise, be lent, re-sold,
hired out or otherwise circulated without the publisher's
prior consent in any form of binding or cover other
than that in which it is published and without a
similar condition including this condition being
imposed on the subsequent purchaser.

All rights reserved. No part of this publication may be
reproduced, stored in a retrieval system, or transmitted,
in any form or by any means, electronic, mechanical,
photocopying, recording or otherwise, without the prior
permission of the publishers.

Contents

Introduction

John and Charles Wesley are the two most influential – and possibly the most extraordinary – religious figures that England has ever produced. In the course of his ministry, John Wesley travelled over a quarter of a million miles on horseback or, as he got older, in a simple coach; he delivered about forty thousand sermons, typically preaching three or four times a day in market squares, outside factory gates, and in farm yards; and he wrote over two hundred books and tracts, mostly composed in the saddle. His younger brother Charles wrote almost five thousand hymns, mostly set to the popular tavern tunes of the day, to be sung at John's open-air meetings. Together they founded the Methodist movement which, after their deaths, broke away from the Anglican Church to which they belonged; and today across the world there are more Methodists than Anglicans. In addition, Charles' hymnody – which enabled everyone to sing God's praises – transformed styles of worship throughout the Western world.

John and Charles were born in 1703 and 1707 respectively, and grew up in the small Lincolnshire town of Epworth. Their father Samuel was the rector, and he and his wife Susanna held strict Puritan views which they instilled into their children with frequent beatings. Susanna tempered her fierce discipline with tender love, devoting herself in the boys' early years to their education; John, in his later ministry, was to display this same combination of toughness and warmth. Samuel, by contrast, showed little compassion for either his children or his parishioners. On one occasion he even paraded an adulteress through the town to shame her, and he frequently accused local farmers of dishonesty. He became so unpopular that a group of farmers came one night and set fire to the rectory; John and Charles narrowly escaped with their lives.

When they reached the age of ten, John and Charles were sent away to school. As a teenager John was priggish and imperious, preferring to harangue younger pupils for their faults than to play with those of his own age. Charles was shy and reserved, his masters complaining that he was too 'dreary'. Both went on to Oxford University. In 1728 Charles experienced a spiritual awakening, which he ascribed to his mother's prayers. Until that moment he had regarded Jesus Christ as a remote, disapproving figure, who threatened eternal punishment; now he became a friend, even a 'lover', who filled his soul with joy. Charles began to spend many hours in fervent prayer, and also to visit the sick and the poor in the city, offering both practical help and spiritual comfort. Soon he attracted to himself a group of other students who wanted to share his new-found devotion. They formed the Holy Club, which later became known as the Methodist Society, because they were so methodical in their prayers and good works.

At his father's insistence, John had been ordained in 1725. At this stage, however, his faith remained cold and filled with fear of divine wrath. He seems to have reacted with envy at Charles' transformation, and insisted on taking over the leadership of the Methodists. This only deepened his self-hatred as he compared his own inner darkness with his brother's spiritual radiance. In 1735 John persuaded Charles to join him on a trip to Georgia in America, with the ostensible purpose of evangelizing the native people. John recorded in his journal that his chief motive 'is the hope of saving my own soul – I hope to learn the true sense of the Gospel by preaching it to the heathen.' His hope was disappointed, and he returned in even greater turmoil: 'I went to America to convert the Indians but, oh, who shall convert me?'

Shortly after landing back in England, John met a Moravian minister, Peter Böhler, who changed his entire understanding of religious faith. Böhler taught that most people regarded faith as an intellectual assent to a series of theological propositions; instead, faith should be understood as an inner movement of the Holy Spirit, which transforms every aspect of the human personality, leading to 'a constant peace'. By detailed reference to the New Testament, Böhler convinced John that this 'free gift of faith' was available to anyone who sought it. John's conversion finally came on 24 May 1738 at a religious meeting in Aldersgate Street, London, as he was listening to an exposition on Paul's Epistle to the Romans: 'I felt my heart strangely warmed; I felt I did trust in Christ, Christ alone for my salvation.'

Now began John's peripatetic ministry, supported by Charles, through which their small Methodist Society spread throughout Britain and America, with branches being formed in virtually every town and in many villages. John's first intention was to preach in parish churches after the normal service. Most parish priests, however, felt threatened by his evangelical fervour, and barred his entry. So he began preaching in the open air, and he soon realized that was the only way to reach the great mass of people who would never visit a church building. Initially success was limited, with few converts. Charles, who frequently joined his brother, recognized that these outdoor meetings needed more emotional stimulus than a sermon alone could provide, and thus began to compose hymns which people could learn instantly. This proved the key: with Charles teaching the crowds to sing, and John telling them how to experience the same spiritual warmth that he enjoyed, hundreds and thousands declared their faith in Christ. John, who was also an adept organizer, formed these converts into groups under the guidance of 'class leaders'; he then trained local preachers to go from group to group expounding the Bible.

John's entries in his journal leading up to his conversion remain the starting point for anyone seeking to grasp the spirit of Methodism, and his account of how the first Methodist group was formed barely a year after his conversion contains his vision for the new movement. A decade later he published a remarkable meditation on the Lord's Prayer, which was really an instruction to his followers on how to pray. Perhaps the most cogent expression of his faith is 'A Plain Account of Genuine Christianity' written in 1753. Despite intense opposition from bishops and clergy, John remained a loyal Anglican throughout his life. However, this did not prevent him from building Methodist chapels, nor from introducing new forms of worship. His most striking innovation was an annual Covenant service, in which people renewed their commitment to Christ; this continues to be the climax of the Methodist calendar.

In 1749 Charles married Sarah Gwynne; and, judging from his poetry, they enjoyed a wonderfully happy union. In the same year, John became engaged to someone whom Charles regarded as quite unsuitable. Charles prevented this marriage by persuading the woman to marry someone else. John was furious, and it led to a permanent estrangement between the two brothers, compelling Charles to withdraw from active leadership of the Methodist societies. Two years later John made a disastrous match with a widow, who quickly came to resent his frequent absences; John reacted by spending even more time on preaching tours.

Happily, Charles continued to write hymns, and John continued to use these hymns at his meetings. Congregational hymn singing had already been introduced in a few independent churches earlier in the century, but the melodies were mostly dull and solemn, and the words heavily theological. Charles not only used popular tunes, but also wrote words that spoke to the heart. As Methodist chapels sprang up across Britain and America, fervent renditions of Charles' hymns echoed round their plain, unadorned walls. Hymn singing only became widespread in parish churches a century later, and it is a credit to Charles' genius that his hymns formed the staple of the new Anglican hymnals. His finest works – such as 'Jesu, lover of my soul', and 'Love divine, all loves excelling' – remain as popular as ever.

In 1783 John Wesley asked the Bishop of London, who was broadly sympathetic to Wesley's evangelism, to ordain 27 Methodist preachers as Anglican priests, so that they could cross the Atlantic and lead Methodism in America. The Bishop refused, and John decided to carry out the ordination himself. Charles was deeply shocked at this action, believing that it would force a split between the Anglican Church and Methodists. Charles was proved right, but the split did not occur until after both brothers had died – Charles in 1788 and John three years later. Throughout his life John had always given to the poor any money he had received, and his instructions for his funeral were consistent with this voluntary poverty. His body was laid out in the cheapest wool; and, instead of a hearse, six unemployed labourers were given a pound each to carry his body to the grave.

ROBERT VAN DE WEYER

Writings of John Wesley:
a Selection (1738–1780)

I

JOHN WESLEY'S JOURNAL:

EXTRACTS FROM 8 JANUARY – 24 MAY 1738

SUNDAY 8 JANUARY

In the fullness of my heart, I wrote the following words:

By the most infallible of proofs, inward feeling, I am convinced:

1. Of unbelief – having no such faith in Christ as will prevent my heart from being troubled, which it could not be if I believed in God and rightly believed also in [Christ];
2. Of pride throughout my life past, inasmuch as I thought I had what I find I have not;
3. Of gross irrecollection, inasmuch as in a storm I cry to God every moment; in a calm, not;
4. Of levity and luxuriancy of spirit, recurring whenever the pressure is taken off; and appearing by my speaking words not tending to edify; but most by my manner of speaking of my enemies.

Lord, save, or I perish! Save me:

1. By such a faith as implies peace in life and in death;
2. By such humility as may fill my heart from this hour forever, with a piercing, uninterrupted sense, *nihil est quod hactenus feci*; (I have done nothing hitherto) having evidently built without a foundation;
3. By such a recollection as may cry to thee every moment, especially when all is calm. Give me faith, or I die; give me a lowly spirit: otherwise, *mihi non sit suave vivere*; (Let life be a burden to me);
4. By steadiness, seriousness, σεμνδτης, sobriety of spirit; avoiding, as fire, every word that tends not to edifying, and never

speaking of any who oppose me; or sin against God, without all my own sins set in array before my face.

TUESDAY 24 JANUARY

We spoke with two ships, outward-bound, from whom we had the welcome news of our wanting but 160 leagues of the Land's End. My mind was now full of thought, part of which I wrote down as follows:

I went to America to convert the Indians but, oh, who shall convert me? Who, what, is he that will deliver me from this evil heart of unbelief? I have a fair summer religion. I can talk well, nay, and believe myself, while no danger is near. But let death look me in the face, and my spirit is troubled. Nor can I say, *to die is gain*.

> I have a sin of fear, that when I've spun
> My last thread, I shall perish on the shore!

I think, verily, if the Gospel be true, I am safe, for I not only have given and do give all my goods to feed the poor; I not only give my body to be burned, drowned, or whatever God shall appoint for me; but I follow after charity (though not as I ought, yet as I can) if haply I may attain it. I *now* believe the Gospel is true. *I show my faith by my works* by staking my all upon it. I would do so again and again a thousand times, if the choice were still to make. Whoever sees me, sees I would be a Christian. Therefore *are my ways not like other men's ways?* Therefore, I have been, I am, I am content to be, a *byword, a proverb of reproach*. But in a storm I think, 'What if the Gospel be not true? Then thou art of all men most foolish. For what have you given up your goods, your ease, your friends, your reputation, your country, your life? For what are you wandering over the face of the earth – a dream, a cunningly devised fable? Oh, who will deliver me from this fear of death? What shall I do? Where shall I fly from it? Should I fight against it by thinking or by not thinking of it?' A wise man advised me some time since, 'Be still and go on.' Perhaps this is best, to look upon it as my cross; when it comes, to let it humble me and quicken all my good resolutions, especially that of praying without ceasing, and at other times to take no thought about it, but quietly go on in the work of the Lord.

1. For many years I have been tossed by various winds of doctrine. I asked long ago, 'What must I do to be saved?' The scripture answered, 'Keep the Commandments, believe, hope, love; follow after these tempers till you have fully attained (that is, till death) by all those outward works and means which God has appointed, by walking as Christ walked.'

2. I was early warned against laying, as the Papists do, too much stress on outward works – or on a faith without works; which, as it does not include, so it will never lead to, true hope or charity. Nor am I sensible that to this hour I have laid too much stress on either; having from the very beginning valued both faith and the means of grace and good works, not on their own account, but as believing that God, who had appointed them, would by them bring me in due time to the mind that was in Christ.

3. But before God's time was come, I fell among some Lutheran and Calvinist authors, whose confused and indigested accounts magnified faith to such an amazing size that it quite hid all the rest of the Commandments. I did not then see that this was the natural effect of their overgrown fear of popery, being so terrified with the cry of merit and good works that they plunged at once into the other extreme. In this labyrinth I was utterly lost, not being able to find out what the error was, nor yet to reconcile this uncouth hypothesis either with scripture or common sense.

4. The English writers, such as Bishop Beveridge, Bishop Taylor and Mr Nelson, a little relieved me from these well-meaning, wrong-headed Germans. Their accounts of Christianity I could easily see to be, in the main, consistent both with reason and scripture. Only when they interpreted scripture in different ways I was often much at a loss. And again, there was one thing much insisted on in scripture – the unity of the Church – which none of them, I thought, clearly explained or strongly inculcated.

5. But it was not long before Providence brought me to those who showed me a sure rule of interpreting scripture, viz: *Consensus veterum: quod ab omnibus, quod ubique, quod semper creditum* (the consensus of antiquity: that which has been believed by everyone, everywhere and always). At the same time they sufficiently insisted upon a due regard to the one Church at all times and in all places.

Nor was it long before I bent the bow too far the other way:

1. By making antiquity a coordinate rather than subordinate rule with scripture.
2. By admitting several doubtful writings as undoubted evidences of antiquity.
3. By extending antiquity too far, even to the middle or end of the fourth century.
4. By believing more practices to have been universal in the ancient Church than ever were so.
5. By not considering that the decrees of one provincial synod could bind only that providence; and that the decrees of a general synod [bound] only those provinces whose representatives met therein.
6. By not considering that the most of those decrees were adapted to particular times and occasions; and consequently, when these occasions ceased, must cease to bind even those provinces.

These considerations insensibly stole upon me as I grew acquainted with the mystic writers, whose noble descriptions of union with God and internal religion made everything else appear mean, flat and insipid. But, in truth, they made good works appear so, too; yea, and faith itself, and what not?

WEDNESDAY 24 MAY

What occurred on Wednesday 24th, I think best to relate at large, after premising what may make it the better understood. Let him that cannot receive it ask the Father of lights that he would give more light both to him and me.

1. I believe, till I was about ten years old, I had not sinned away that washing of the Holy Ghost which was given me in baptism, having been strictly educated and carefully taught that I could only be saved by universal obedience, by keeping all the commandments of God – in the meaning of which I was diligently instructed. And those instructions, so far as they respected outward duties and sins, I gladly received and often thought of. But all that was said to me of inward obedience or holiness I neither understood nor remembered. So that I was indeed as ignorant of the true meaning of the law as I was of the Gospel of Christ.

2. The next six or seven years were spent at school, where, outward restraints being removed, I was much more negligent than before, even of outward duties, and almost continually guilty of outward sins which I knew to be such, though they were not scandalous in the eye of the world. However, I still read the scriptures and said my prayers, morning and evening. And what I now hoped to be saved by was (i) not being so bad as other people; (ii) having still a kindness for religion; and (iii) reading the Bible, going to church and saying my prayers.

3. Being removed to the university for five years, I still said my prayers both in public and in private, and read with the scriptures several other books of religion, especially comments on the New Testament. Yet I had not all this while so much as a notion of inward holiness; nay, went on habitually, and for the most part very contentedly, in some or other known sin – indeed, with some intermissions and short struggles, especially before and after the Holy Communion, which I was obliged to receive thrice a year. I cannot well tell what I hoped to be saved by now, when I was continually sinning against that little light I had, unless by those transient fits of what many divines taught me to call 'repentance'.

4. When I was about 22, my father pressed me to enter into Holy Orders. At the same time, the providence of God directing me to Kempis's *Christian Pattern*, I began to see that true religion was seated in the heart and that God's law extended to all our thoughts as well as words and actions. I was, however, very angry at Kempis for

being *too strict*, though I read him only in Dean Stanhope's translation. Yet I had frequently much sensible comfort in reading him, such as I was an utter stranger to before. Meeting likewise with a religious friend, which I never had till now, I began to alter the whole form of my conversation, and to set in earnest upon 'a new life'. I set apart an hour or two a day for religious retirement. I communicated every week. I watched against all sin, whether in word or deed. I began to aim at, and pray for, inward holiness. So that now, *doing so much and living so good a life*, I doubted not but I was a good Christian.

5. Removing soon after to another college, I executed a resolution which I was before convinced was of the utmost importance – shaking off at once all my trifling acquaintance. I began to see more and more the value of time. I applied myself closer to study. I watched more carefully against actual sins; I advised others to be religious, according to that scheme of religion by which I modelled my own life. But meeting now with Mr Law's *Christian Perfection* and *Serious Call* (although I was much offended at many parts of both, yet) they convinced me more than ever of the exceeding height and breadth and depth of the law of God. The light flowed in so mightily upon my soul that everything appeared in a new view. I cried to God for help and resolved not to prolong the time of obeying him, as I had never done before. And by my continued *endeavour to keep his whole law*, inward and outward, *to the utmost of my power*, I was persuaded that I should be accepted of him and that I was even then in a state of salvation.

6. In 1730 I began visiting the prisons, assisting the poor and sick in town, and doing what other good I could by my presence or my little fortune to the bodies and souls of all men. To this end I abridged myself of all superfluities, and many that are called necessaries of life. I soon became a *byword* for so doing, and I rejoiced that *my name was cast out as evil*. The next spring I began observing the Wednesday and Friday fasts commonly observed in the ancient Church, tasting no food till three in the afternoon. And now I knew not how to go any further. I diligently strove against all sin. I omitted

no sort of self-denial which I thought lawful. I carefully used, both in public and private, all the means of grace at all opportunities. I omitted no occasion of doing good. I for that reason suffered evil. And all this I knew to be nothing unless as it was directed toward inward holiness. Accordingly this, the image of God, was what I aimed at in all, by doing his will, not my own. Yet when, after continuing some years in this course, I apprehended myself to be near death, I could not find that all this gave me any comfort or any assurance of acceptance with God. At this I was then not a little surprised, not imagining I had been all this time building on the sand, nor considering that *other foundation can no man lay than that which is laid by God, even Christ Jesus*.

7. Soon after, a contemplative man convinced me still more than I was convinced before that outward works are nothing, being alone; and in several conversations instructed me how to pursue inward holiness, or a union of the soul with God. But even of his instructions (though I then received them as the words of God) I cannot but now observe (a) that he spoke so incautiously against *trusting* in *outward works* that he discouraged me from *doing* them at all; (b) that he recommended (as it were, to supply what was wanting in them) *mental prayer* and the like exercises, as the most effectual means of purifying the soul and uniting it with God. Now these were, in truth, as much *my own works* as visiting the sick or clothing the naked; and the 'union with God' thus pursued was as really *my own righteousness* as any I had before pursued under another name.

8. In this *refined* way of trusting to my own works and my own righteousness (so zealously inculcated by the mystic writers), I dragged on heavily, finding no comfort or help therein till the time of my leaving England. On shipboard, however, I was again active in outward works, where it pleased God of his free mercy to give me 26 of the Moravian brethren for companions, who endeavoured to show me a more excellent way. But I understood it not at first. I was too learned and too wise, so that it seemed foolishness unto me. And I continued preaching and following after, and trusting in that righteousness whereby no flesh can be justified.

9. All the time I was at Savannah I was thus beating the air. Being ignorant of the righteousness of Christ, which, by a living faith in him, bringeth salvation *to every one that believeth*. I sought to establish my own righteousness, and so laboured in the fire all my days. I was now properly *under the law*. I knew that *the law* of God was *spiritual; I consented to it that it was good*. Yea, *I delighted in it after the inner man*. Yet was I *carnal, sold under sin*. Every day was I constrained to cry out, *What I do, I allow not: for what I would, I do not; but what I hate, that I do. To will is indeed present with me; but how to perform that which is good, I find not. For the good which I would, I do not, but the evil which I would not, that I do. I find a law that when I would do good, evil is present with me, even the law in my members, warring against the law of my mind and still bringing me into captivity to the law of sin.*

10. In this state I was indeed fighting continually, but not conquering. Before, I had willingly served sin; now it was unwillingly, but still I served it. I fell and rose and fell again. Sometimes I was overcome and in heaviness: sometimes I overcame and was in joy. For as in the former state I had some foretastes of the terrors of the law, so had I in this of the comforts of the Gospel. During this whole struggle between nature and grace which had now continued above ten years, I had many remarkable returns to prayer, especially when I was in trouble. I had many sensible comforts, which are indeed no other than short anticipations of the life of faith. But I was still *under the law*, not *under grace* (the state most who are called Christians are content to live and die in), for I was only *striving with*, not *freed from*, *sin*. Neither had I *the witness of the Spirit with my spirit*, and indeed could not, for I *sought it not by faith, but as it were by the works of the law*.

11. In my return to England, January 1738, being in imminent danger of death and very uneasy on that account, I was strongly convinced that the cause of that uneasiness was unbelief and that the gaining a true, living faith was the one thing needful for me. But still I fixed not this faith on its right object: I meant only faith in God, not faith in or through Christ. Again, I knew not that I was *wholly void of*

this faith but only thought *I had not enough* of it. So that when Peter Böhler, whom God prepared for me as soon as I came to London, affirmed of true faith in Christ (which is but one) that it had those two fruits inseparably attending it, 'dominion over sin, and constant peace from a sense of forgiveness', I was quite amazed and looked upon it as a new Gospel. If this was so, it was clear I had not faith. But I was not willing to be convinced of this. Therefore I disputed with all my might and laboured to prove that faith might be where these were not, especially where the sense of forgiveness was not; for all the scriptures relating to this I had been long since taught to construe away and to call all Presbyterians who spoke otherwise. Besides, I well saw no one could, in the nature of things, have such a sense of forgiveness and not *feel* it. But I felt it not. If, then, there was no faith without this, all my pretensions to faith dropped at once.

12. When I met Peter Böhler again, he consented to put the dispute upon the issue which I desired, namely, scripture and experience. I first consulted the scripture. But when I set aside the glosses of men and simply considered the words of God, comparing them together, endeavouring to illustrate the obscure by the plainer passages, I found they all made against me and was forced to retreat to my last hold, 'that experience would never agree with the *literal interpretation* of those scriptures. Nor could I therefore allow it to be true, till I found some living witnesses of it'. He replied he could show me such at any time; if I desired it, the next day. And, accordingly, the next day he came again with three others, all of whom testified of their own personal experience that a true living faith in Christ is inseparable from a sense of pardon for all past, and freedom from all present, sins. They added with one mouth that this faith was the gift, the free gift of God, and that he would surely bestow it upon every soul who earnestly and perseveringly sought it. I was now thoroughly convinced and, by the grace of God, I resolved to seek it unto the end, first, by absolutely renouncing all dependence, in whole or in part, upon *my own* works or righteousness – on which I had really grounded my hope of salvation, though I knew it not, from my youth up; second, by adding to 'the constant use of all the

"other" means of grace', continual prayer for this very thing – justifying, saving faith, a full reliance on the blood of Christ shed for *me*, a trust in him, as *my* Christ, as *my* sole justification, sanctification, and redemption.

13. I continued thus to seek it (though with strange indifference, dullness and coldness and unusually frequent relapses into sin) till Wednesday, May 24. I think it was about five this morning, that I opened my Testament on those words, τἀ μέγιστα ἡμῖν καὶ τίμια ἐπαγγέλματα δεδώρηται, ἱνὰ [διὰ τοΰτων] γένησθε θείας κοινωνοι φΰσεως, *There are given unto us exceeding great and precious promises, even that you should be partakers of the divine nature* (2 Peter 1:4). Just as I went out, I opened it again on those words, *You are not far from the kingdom of God*. In the afternoon I was asked to go to St Paul's. The anthem was *Out of the deep have I called unto you, O Lord: Lord, hear my voice. O let your ears consider well the voice of my complaint. If you, Lord, will be extreme to mark what is done amiss, O Lord, who may abide it? For there is mercy with you; therefore shall you be feared. O Israel, trust in the Lord, for with the Lord there is mercy and with him is plenteous redemption. And he shall redeem Israel from all his sins.*

14. In the evening, I went very unwillingly to a society in Aldersgate Street, where one was reading Luther's Preface to the Epistle to the Romans. About a quarter before nine, while he was describing the change which God works in the heart through faith in Christ, I felt my heart strangely warmed. I felt I did trust in Christ, Christ alone for salvation; and an assurance was given me that he had taken away *my* sins, even *mine*, and saved *me* from the law of sin and death.

15. I began to pray with all my might for those who had in a more especial manner despitefully used me and persecuted me. I then testified openly to all there what I now first felt in my heart. But it was not long before the enemy suggested, 'This cannot be faith, for where is your joy?' Then was I taught that 'peace and victory over sin are essential to faith in the Captain of our salvation but that, as to the transports of joy – that usually attend the beginning of it especially

in those who have mourned deeply – God sometimes giveth, sometimes withholdest them, according to the counsels of his own will'.

16. After my return home, I was much buffeted with temptations, but cried out and they fled away. They returned again and again. I as often lifted up my eyes and he *sent me help from his holy place*. And herein I found [in what] the difference between this and my former state chiefly consisted. I was striving, yea, fighting with all my might under the law, as well as under grace. But then I was sometimes, if not often, conquered; now, I was always conqueror.

II

The Nature, Design and General Rules of the Methodist Societies

1. In the latter end of the year 1739, eight or ten persons came to me in London, who appeared to be deeply convinced of sin, and earnestly groaning for redemption. They desired (as did two or three more the next day) that I would spend some time with them in prayer, and advise them how to flee from the wrath to come; which they saw continually hanging over their heads. That we might have more time for this great work, I appointed a day when they might all come together, which from thenceforward they did every week, namely, on Thursday, in the evening. To these, and as many more as desired to join with them (for their number increased daily), I gave those advices, from time to time, which I judged most needful for them; and we always concluded our meeting with prayer suited to their several necessities.

2. This was the rise of the United Society, first in London, and then in other places. Such a society is no other than 'a company of men having the form and seeking the power of godliness, united in order to pray together, to receive the word of exhortation, and to watch over one another in love, that they may help each other to work out their salvation'.

3. That it may the more easily be discerned, whether they are indeed working out their own salvation, each society is divided into smaller companies, called *classes*, according to their respective places of abode. There are about 12 persons in every class; one of whom is styled *the Leader*. It is his business (a) to see each person in his class once a week at least, in order to inquire how their souls prosper; to advise, reprove, comfort, or exhort, as occasion may require; to receive what they are willing to give toward the relief of the poor; (b)

to meet the Minister and the Stewards of the society once a week; in order to inform the Minister of any that are sick, or of any that walk disorderly, and will not be reproved; to pay to the Stewards what they have received of their several classes in the week preceding; and to show their account of what each person has contributed.

4. There is only one condition previously required in those who desire admission into these societies – a desire *to flee from the wrath to come, to be saved from their sins*: but, wherever this is really fixed in the soul, it will be shown by its fruits. It is therefore expected of all who continue therein that they should continue to evidence their desire of salvation:

First, by doing no harm, by avoiding evil in every kind; especially that which is most generally practised: such is, the taking the name of God in vain; the profaning the day of the Lord, either by doing ordinary work thereon or by buying or selling; drunkenness, buying or selling spirituous liquors, or drinking them, unless in cases of extreme necessity; fighting, quarrelling, brawling; brother going to law with brother; returning evil for evil, or railing for railing; the using many words in buying or selling; the buying or selling uncustomed goods; the giving or taking things on usury, that is unlawful interest; uncharitable or unprofitable conversation, particularly speaking evil of Magistrates or of Ministers; doing to others as we would not they should do unto us; doing what we know is not for the glory of God, as the 'putting on of gold or costly apparel'; the taking such diversions as cannot be used in the name of the Lord Jesus; the singing those songs, or reading those books, which do not tend to the knowledge or love of God; softness, and needless self-indulgence; laying up treasures upon earth; borrowing without a probability of paying; or taking up goods without a probability of paying for them.

5. It is expected of all who continue in these societies that they should continue to evidence their desire of salvation:

Secondly, by doing good, by being, in every kind, merciful after their power; as they have opportunity, doing good of every possible sort, and as far as is possible, to all men; to their bodies, of the ability which God giveth, by giving food to the hungry, by clothing the naked, by visiting or helping them that are sick, or in prison; to their souls, by instructing, reproving, or exhorting all they have any intercourse with; trampling under foot that enthusiastic doctrine of devils, that 'we are not to do good unless our heart be free to it'; by doing good especially to them that are of the household of faith, or groaning so to be; employing them preferably to others, buying one of another; helping each other in business; and so much the more, because the world will love its own, and them only; by all possible diligence and frugality, that the Gospel be not blamed; by running with patience the race that is set before them, *denying themselves, and taking up their cross daily*; submitting to bear the reproach of Christ, to be as the filth and offscouring of the world; and looking that men should *say all manner of evil of them falsely for the Lord's sake*.

6. It is expected of all who desire to continue in these societies that they should continue to evidence their desire of salvation:

Thirdly, by attending upon all the ordinances of God. Such are the public worship of God; the ministry of the Word, either read or expounded; the supper of the Lord; family and private prayer; searching the scriptures; and fasting, or abstinence.

7. These are the General Rules of our societies; all which we are taught of God to observe, even in his written Word, the only rule, and the sufficient rule, both of our faith and practice. And all these, we know, his Spirit writes on every truly awakened heart. If there be any among us who observe them not, who habitually break any of them, let it be made known unto them who watch over that soul as they that must give an account. We will admonish him of the error of his ways, we will bear with him for a season; but then if he repent not, he hath no more place among us. We have delivered our own souls.

1743

III

A Meditation on the Lord's Prayer

1. After having taught the true nature and ends of prayer, our Lord subjoins an example of it; even that divine form of prayer which seems in this place to be proposed by way of pattern chiefly, as the model and standard of all our prayers: *after this manner therefore pray yet*. Whereas, elsewhere he enjoins the use of these very words: *He said unto them, When you pray, say*... (Luke 11:2).

2. We may observe, in general, concerning this divine prayer, first, that it contains all we can reasonably or innocently pray for. There is nothing which we have need to ask of God, nothing which we can ask without offending him, which is not included, either directly or indirectly, in this comprehensive form. Secondly, that it contains all we can reasonably or innocently desire; whatever is for the glory of God, whatever is needful or profitable, not only for ourselves, but for every creature in heaven and earth. And, indeed, our prayers are the proper test of our desires; nothing being fit to have a place in our desires which is not fit to have a place in our prayers: what we may not pray for, neither should we desire. Thirdly, that it contains all our duty to God and man; whatsoever things are pure and holy, whatsoever God requires of the children of men, whatsoever is acceptable in his sight, whatsoever it is whereby we may profit our neighbour, being expressed or implied therein.

3. It consists of three parts – the preface, the petitions, and the doxology, or conclusion. The preface, *Our Father, who are in heaven*, lays a general foundation for prayer; comprising what we must first know of God before we can pray in confidence of being heard. It likewise points out to us all those tempers with which we are to

approach to God, which are most essentially requisite, if we desire either our prayers or our lives should find acceptance with him.

4. *Our Father*: If he is a Father, then he is good, then he is loving, to his children. And here is the first and great reason for prayer. God is willing to bless; let us ask for a blessing. *Our Father*: our Creator; the Author of our being; he who raised us from the dust of the earth; who breathed into us the breath of life, and we became living souls. But if he made us, let us ask, and he will not withhold any good thing from the work of his own hands. *Our Father*: our Preserver; who, day by day, sustains the life he has given; of whose continuing love we now and every moment receive life and breath and all things. So much the more boldly let us come to him, and we shall *obtain mercy, and find grace to help in time of need.* Above all, the Father of our Lord Jesus Christ, and of all that believe in him; who justifies us *freely by his grace, through the redemption that is in Jesus*; who has *blotted out all our sins, and healed all our infirmities*; who has received us for his own children, by adoption and grace; and *because* we *are sons, has sent forth the Spirit of his Son into* our *hearts, crying, Abba, Father*; who *has begotten us again of incorruptible seed*, and *created us anew in Christ Jesus.* Therefore we know that he hears us always; therefore we pray to him without ceasing. We pray, because we love; and *we love him because he first loved us.*

5. *Our Father*: Not *mine* only who now cry unto him, but *ours* in the most extensive sense. The God and *Father of the spirits of all flesh*; the Father of angels and men: so the very Heathens acknowledge him to be, Πατὴρ ἀυδρῶυ τε θεῶυ τε. The Father of the universe, of all the families both in heaven and earth. Therefore with him there is no respect of persons. He loves all that he has made. *He is loving unto every man, and his mercy is over all his works.* And the Lord's delight is in them that fear him, and put their trust in his mercy; in them that trust in him through the Son of his love, knowing they are *accepted in the Beloved*. But *if God so loved us, we ought also to love one another*; yea, all mankind; seeing *God so loved the world that he gave his only begotten Son*, even to die the death, that they *might not perish, but have everlasting life.*

6. *Who are in heaven*: High and lifted up, God over all, blessed forever: who, sitting on the circle of the heavens, beholds all things both in heaven and earth; whose eye pervades the whole sphere of created being; yea, and of uncreated night; unto whom *are known all his works*, and all the works of every creature, not only *from the beginning of the world* (a poor, low, weak translation) but ἀπ' αἰωνος, from all *eternity*, from everlasting to everlasting; who constrains the host of heaven, as well as the children of men, to cry out with wonder and amazement, Oh, the depth! *The depth of the riches, both of the wisdom and of the knowledge of God! Who are in heaven*: The Lord and Ruler of all, superintending and disposing all things; who are the King of kings, and Lord of lords, the blessed and only Potentate; who are strong and girded about with power, doing whatsoever pleases you; the Almighty; for whensoever you will, to do is present with you. *In heaven*: eminently there. Heaven is your throne, *the place where your honour* particularly *dwells*. But not there alone; for you fill heaven and earth, the whole expanse of space. *Heaven and earth are full of your glory. Glory be to you, O Lord most high!*

Therefore should we *serve the Lord with fear, and rejoice unto him with reverence.* Therefore should we think, speak, and act, as continually under the eye, in the immediate presence, of the Lord, the King.

7. *Hallowed be your name.* This is the first of the six petitions, whereof the prayer itself is composed. The name of God is God himself, the nature of God so far as it can be discovered to man. It means therefore, together with his existence, all his attributes or perfections: his Eternity, particularly signified by his great and incommunicable name, JEHOVAH, as the Apostle John translates it: *The Alpha and Omega, the beginning and the end; he which is, and which was, and which is to come*; his Fullness of Being, denoted by his other great name, *I AM THAT I AM!* – his omnipresence – his omnipotence; who is indeed the only agent in the material world; all matter being essentially dull and inactive, and moving only as it is moved by the finger of God; and he is the spring of action in every creature, visible and invisible, which could neither act nor exist

without the continual influx and agency of his almighty power; his wisdom, clearly deduced from the things that are seen, from the goodly order of the universe; his Trinity in Unity, and Unity in Trinity, discovered to us in the very first line of his written word; literally, *the Gods created*, a plural noun joined with a verb of the singular number; as well as in every part of his subsequent revelations, given by the mouth of all of his holy Prophets and Apostles; his essential purity and holiness; and, above all, his love, which is the very brightness of his glory.

In praying that God, or his name, may be hallowed or glorified, we pray that he may be known, such as he is, by all that are capable thereof, by all intelligent beings, and with affections suitable to that knowledge; that he may be duly honoured, and feared, and loved, by all in heaven above and in the earth beneath; by all angels and men, whom for that end he has made capable of knowing and loving him to eternity.

8. *Your kingdom come.* This has a close connection with the preceding petition. In order that the name of God might be hallowed, we pray that his kingdom, the kingdom of Christ, may come. This kingdom then comes to a particular person, when he *repents and believes the Gospel*; when he is taught of God, not only to know himself, but to know Jesus Christ and him crucified. As *this is life eternal, to know the only true God, and Jesus Christ whom he hath sent*; so it is the kingdom of God begun below, set up in the believer's heart; *the Lord God Omnipotent* then *reigns*, when he is known through Christ Jesus. He takes unto himself his mighty power, that he may subdue all things unto himself. He goes on in the soul conquering and to conquer, till he has put all things under his feet, till *every thought is brought into captivity to the obedience of Christ.*

When therefore God shall *give his Son the Heathen for his inheritance, and the uttermost parts of the earth for his possession*; when *all kingdoms shall bow before him, and all nations shall do him service*; when *the mountain of the Lord's house*, the Church of Christ, *shall be established in the top of the mountains*; when *the fullness of the Gentiles shall come in, and all Israel shall be saved*; then shall it be seen that *the*

Lord is King, and has put on glorious apparel, appearing to every soul of man as King of kings and Lord of lords. And it is meet for all those who love his appearing to pray that he would hasten the time; that this his kingdom, the kingdom of grace, may come quickly, and swallow up all the kingdoms of the earth; that all mankind, receiving him for their King, truly believing in his name, may be filled with righteousness, and peace, and joy, with holiness and happiness, till they are removed hence into his heavenly kingdom, there to reign with him forever and ever.

For this also we pray in those words, *Your kingdom come*: we pray for the coming of his everlasting kingdom, the kingdom of glory in heaven, which is the continuation and perfection of the kingdom of grace on earth. Consequently this, as well as the preceding petition, is offered up for the whole intelligent creation, who are all interested in this grand event, the final renovation of all things, by God's putting an end to misery and sin, to infirmity and death, taking all things into his own hands, and setting up the kingdom which endures throughout all ages.

Exactly answerable to all this are those awful words in the prayer at the burial of the dead: 'Beseeching you; that it may please you of your gracious goodness, shortly to accomplish the number of your elect, and to hasten your kingdom; that we, with all those that are departed in the true faith of your holy name, may have our perfect consummation and bliss, both in body and soul, in your everlasting glory.'

9. *Your will be done in earth, as it is in heaven*. This is the necessary and immediate consequence whereever the kingdom of God is come; wherever God dwells in the soul by faith, and Christ reigns in the heart by love.

It is probable that many, perhaps the generality of men, at the first view of these words, are apt to imagine they are only an expression of, or petition for, resignation; for a readiness to suffer the will of God, whatsoever it be, concerning us. And this is unquestionably a divine and excellent temper, a most precious gift of God. But this is not what we pray for in this petition; at least, not in the chief and primary sense of it. We pray, not so much for a passive, as for an active, conformity to the will of God, in saying, *Your will be done in earth, as it is in heaven.*

How is it done by the angels of God in heaven, those who now circle in his throne rejoicing? They do it *willingly*; they love his commandments, and gladly hearken to his words. It is their meat and drink to do his will; it is their highest glory and joy. They do it *continually*; there is no interruption in their willing service. They rest not day or night, but employ every hour (speaking after the manner of men; otherwise our measures of duration, days, and nights, and hours, have no place in eternity) in fulfilling his commands, in executing his designs, in performing the counsel of his will. And they do it *perfectly*. No sin, no defect belongs to angelic minds. It is true, *the stars are not pure in his sight*, even the morning stars that sing together before him. *In his sight*, that is, in comparison of him, the very angels are not pure. But this does not imply that they are not pure in *themselves*. Doubtless they are; they are without spot and blameless. They are altogether devoted to his will, and perfectly obedient in all things.

If we view this in another light, we may observe the angels of God in heaven do *all* the will of God. And they do nothing else, nothing but what they are absolutely assured is his will. Again, they do all the will of God *as* willed; in the manner which pleases him, and no other. Yea, and they do this only *because* it is his will; for this end, and no other reason.

10. When therefore we pray that the will of God may *be done in earth as it is in heaven*, the meaning is that all the inhabitants of the earth, even the whole race of mankind, may do the will of their Father which is in heaven, as *willingly* as the holy angels; that these may do it *continually*, even as they, without any interruption of their willing service; yea and that they may do it *perfectly*, that 'the God of peace, through the blood of the everlasting covenant, may make them perfect in every good work to do his will, and work in them' all 'which is well-pleasing in his sight'.

In other words, we pray that we and all mankind may do the whole will of God in all things, and nothing else; not the least thing but what is the holy and acceptable will of God. We pray they we may do the whole will of God as he wills, in the manner that pleases him; and lastly, that we may do it *because* it is his will; that this may be the sole reason and ground, the whole and only motive, of whatsoever we think, or whatsoever we speak or do.

11. *Give us this day our daily bread.* In the three former petitions we have been praying for all mankind. We come now more particularly to desire a supply for our own wants. Not that we are directed, even here, to confine our prayer altogether to ourselves; but this, and each of the following petitions, may be used for the whole Church of Christ upon earth.

By 'bread' we may understand all things needful, whether for our souls or bodies – the things pertaining to life and godliness: We understand not barely the outward bread, what our Lord terms *the meat which perisheth*; but much more the spiritual bread, the grace of God, the food *which endures unto everlasting life.* It was the judgement of many of the ancient Fathers that we are here to understand the sacramental bread also; daily received in the beginning by the whole Church of Christ, and highly esteemed, till the love of many waxed cold, as the grand channel whereby the grace of his Spirit was conveyed to the souls of all the children of God.

Our daily bread. The word we render *daily* has been differently explained by different commentators. But the most plain and natural sense of it seems to be this, which is retained in almost all translations, as well ancient as modern: what is sufficient for this day, and so for each day as it succeeds.

12. *Give us*: For we claim nothing of right, but only of free mercy. We deserve not the air we breathe, the earth that bears, or the sun that shines upon us. All our desert, we own, is hell; but God loves us freely – therefore, we ask him to give what we can no more procure for ourselves, than we can merit it at his hands.

Not that either the goodness or the power of God is a reason for us to stand idle. It is his will that we should use all diligence in all things, that we should employ our utmost endeavours, as much as if our success were the natural effect of our own wisdom and strength;

and then, as though we had done nothing, we are to depend on Him, the giver of every good and perfect gift.

This day: For we are to take no thought for the morrow. For this very end has our wise Creator divided life into these little portions of time, so clearly separated from each other that we might look on every day as a fresh gift of God, another life, which we may devote to his glory; and that every evening may be as the close of life, beyond which we are to see nothing but eternity.

13. *And forgive us our trespasses, as we forgive them that trespass against us.* As nothing but sin can hinder the bounty of God from flowing forth upon every creature, so this petition naturally follows the former; that, all hindrances being removed, we may the more clearly trust in the God of love for every manner of thing which is good.

Our trespasses: The word properly signifies *our debts.* Thus our sins are frequently represented in scripture; every sin laying us under a fresh debt to God, to whom we already owe, as it were, ten thousand talents. What, then, can we answer when he shall say, *Pay me that you owe*? We are utterly insolvent; we have nothing to pay; we have wasted all our substance. Therefore, if he deal with us according to the rigour of his law, if he exact what he justly may, he must command us to be *bound hand and foot, and delivered over to the tormentors.*

Indeed, we are already bound hand and foot by the chains of our own sins. These, considered with regard to ourselves, are chains of iron and fetters of brass. They are wounds wherewith the world, the flesh, and the devil have gashed and mangled us all over. They are diseases that drink up our blood and spirits, that bring us down to the chambers of the grave. But, considered as they are here, with regard to God, they are debts immense and numberless. Well, therefore, seeing we have nothing to pay, may we cry unto Him, that he would frankly forgive us all!

The word translated *forgive* implies either to forgive a debt, or to unloose a chain. And, if we attain the former, the latter follows of course; if our debts are forgiven, the chains fall off our hands. As soon as ever, through the free grace of God in Christ, we *receive forgiveness of sins*, we receive likewise *a lot among those which are sanctified, by faith which is in him.* Sin has lost its power; it has no dominion over those who are under grace, that is, in favour with God. As *there is now no condemnation to them that are in Christ Jesus*, so they are freed from sin as well as from guilt. *The righteousness of the law is fulfilled in* them, and they *walk not after the flesh but after the Spirit.*

14. *As we forgive them that trespass against us.* In these words our Lord clearly declares both on what condition, and in what degree or manner, we may look to be forgiven of God. All our trespasses and sins are forgiven us, *if* we forgive, and *as* we forgive, others. This is a point of the utmost importance. And our blessed Lord is so jealous lest at any time we should let it slip out of our thoughts that he not only inserts it in the body of his prayer, but presently after repeats it twice over. *If*, says he, *you forgive men their trespasses, your heavenly Father will also forgive you; but if you forgive not men their trespasses, neither will your Father forgive your trespasses* (verses 14, 15). Secondly, God forgives us *as* we forgive others. So that if any malice or bitterness, if any taint of unkindness or anger remains, if we do not clearly, fully, and from the heart forgive all men their trespasses, we so far cut short the forgiveness of our own; God cannot clearly and fully forgive us: He may show us some degree of mercy, but we will not suffer him to blot out all our sins, and forgive all our iniquities.

In the meantime, while we do not from our hearts forgive our neighbour his trespasses, what manner of prayer are we offering to God whenever we utter these words? We are indeed setting God at open defiance; we are daring him to do his worst. *Forgive us our trespasses, as we forgive them that trespass against us.* That is, in plain terms, 'Do not forgive us at all; we desire no favour at your hands. We pray that you will keep our sins in remembrance, and that your wrath may abide upon us.' But can you seriously offer such a prayer to God? And has he not yet cast you quick into hell? Oh, tempt him no longer! Now, even now, by his grace, forgive as you would be forgiven! Now have compassion on your fellow servant, as God has had, and will have, pity on you!

15. *And lead us not into temptation, but deliver us from evil.*

And lead us not into temptation. The word translated *temptation* means trial of any kind. And so the English word temptation was formerly taken in an indifferent sense, although now it is usually understood of solicitation to sin. St James uses the word in both these senses; first, in its general, then in its restrained, acceptation. He takes it in the former sense when he says, *Blessed is the man that endures temptation: For when he is tried,* or approved of God, *he shall receive the crown of life* (James 1:12, 13). He immediately adds, taking the word in the latter sense, *Let no man say, when he is tempted, I am tempted of God: For God cannot be tempted with evil, neither tempts he any man: But every man is tempted when he is drawn away of his own lust,* or *desire,* ἐξελκόμευος – drawn out of God, in whom alone he is safe – *and enticed*; caught as a fish with bait. Then it is, when he is thus *drawn away and enticed,* that he properly enters into temptation. Then temptation covers him as a cloud; it overspreads his whole soul. Then how hardly shall he escape out of the snare! Therefore, we beseech God *not to lead us into temptation*, that is (seeing God tempts no man), not to suffer us to be led into it.

But deliver us from evil: Rather, *from the evil one,* απὸ τοῦ ποτηρου. 'Ο πουηρος is unquestionably *the wicked one*, emphatically so called, the prince and god of this world, who works with mighty power in the children of disobedience. But all those who are the children of God by faith are delivered out of his hands. He may fight against them; and so he will. But he cannot conquer, unless they betray their own souls. He may torment for a time, but he cannot destroy; for God is on their side, who will not fail, in the end, to *avenge his own elect, that cry unto him day and night.* Lord, when we are tempted, suffer us not to enter into temptation! Do you make a way for us to escape that the wicked one touch us not!

16. The conclusion of this divine prayer, commonly called the Doxology, is a solemn thanksgiving, a compendious acknowledgement of the attributes and works of God. *For yours is the kingdom* – the sovereign right of all things that are, or ever were, created; yes, your kingdom is an everlasting kingdom, and your dominion

endures throughout all ages. *The power* – the executive power whereby you govern all things in your everlasting kingdom, whereby you do whatsoever pleases you, in all places of your dominion. *And the glory* – the praise due from every creature, for your power, and the mightiness of your kingdom, and for all your wondrous works which you work from everlasting, and shall do, world without end, *forever and ever*! *Amen*! So be it!

1748

IV

A PLAIN ACCOUNT OF GENUINE CHRISTIANITY

SECTION I

1. I would consider, first, who is a Christian indeed? What does that term properly imply? It has been so long abused, I fear, not only to mean nothing at all, but what was far worse than nothing, to be a cloak for the vilest hypocrisy, for the grossest abominations and immoralities of every kind, that it is high time to rescue it out of the hands of wretches that are a reproach to human nature, to show determinately what manner of man he is to whom this name of right belongs.

2. A 'Christian' cannot think of the Author of his being without abasing himself before him, without a deep sense of the distance between a worm of earth and him that *sits on the circle of the heavens.* In his presence he sinks into the dust, knowing himself to be less than nothing in his eye and being conscious, in a manner words cannot express, of his own littleness, ignorance, foolishness. So that he can only cry out, from the fullness of his heart, 'O God, what is man? What am I?'.

3. He has a continual sense of his dependence on the parent of good, for his being and all the blessings that attend it. To him he refers every natural and every moral endowment, with all that is commonly ascribed either to fortune or to the wisdom, courage, or merit of the possessor. And hence he acquiesces in whatsoever appears to be his will, not only with patience but with thankfulness. He willingly resigns all he is, all he has, to his wise and gracious disposal. The ruling temper of his heart is the most absolute submission and the tenderest gratitude to his sovereign benefactor. And this grateful love creates filial fear, an awful reverence toward him

and an earnest care not to give place to any disposition, not to admit an action, word, or thought, which might in any degree displease that indulgent power to whom he owes his life, breath, and all things.

4. And as he has the strongest affection for the fountain of all good, so he has the firmest confidence in him; a confidence which neither pleasure nor pain, nor life and death, can shake. But yet this, far from creating sloth or indolence, pushes him on to the most vigorous industry. It causes him to put forth all his strength in obeying him in whom he confides; so that he is never faint in his mind, never weary of doing whatever he believes to be his will. And as he knows the most acceptable worship of God is to imitate him he worships, so he is continually labouring to transcribe into himself all his imitable perfections: in particular, his justice, mercy, and truth, so eminently displayed in all his creatures.

5. Above all, remembering that God is love, he is conformed to the same likeness. He is full of love to his neighbour: of universal love, not confined to one sect or party, not restrained to those who agree with him in opinions, or in outward modes of worship, or to those who are allied to him by blood or recommended by nearness of place. Neither does he love those only that love him, or that are endeared to him by intimacy of acquaintance. But his love resembles that of him whose mercy is over all his works. It soars above all these scanty bounds, embracing neighbours and strangers, friends and enemies; yes, not only the good and gentle but also the froward, the evil and unthankful. For he loves every soul that God has made, every child of man, of whatever place or nation. And yet this universal benevolence does in nowise interfere with a peculiar regard for his relations, friends, and benefactors, a fervent love for his country and the most endeared affection to all men of integrity, of clear and generous virtue.

6. His love to these, so to all mankind, is in itself generous and disinterested, springing from no view of advantage to himself, from no regard to profit or praise; no, nor even the pleasure of loving. This is the daughter, not the parent, of his affection. By experience he knows that *social love* (if it mean the love of our neighbour) is absolutely, essentially different from *self-love*, even of the most allowable kind,

just as different as the objects at which they point. And yet it is sure that, if they are under due regulations, each will give additional force to the other, 'till they mix together never to be divided.

7. And this universal, disinterested love is productive of all right affections. It is fruitful of gentleness, tenderness, sweetness; of humanity, courtesy, and affability. It makes a Christian rejoice in the virtues of all, and bear a part in their happiness at the same time that he sympathizes with their pains and compassionates their infirmities. It creates modesty, condescension, prudence – together with calmness and evenness of temper. It is the parent of generosity, openness, and frankness, void of jealousy and suspicion. It begets candour and willingness to believe and hope whatever is kind and friendly of every man; and invincible patience, never overcome of evil, but overcoming evil with good.

8. The same love constrains him to converse not only with a strict regard to truth but with artless sincerity and genuine simplicity, as one in whom there is no guile. And not content with abstaining from all such expressions as are contrary to justice or truth, he endeavours to refrain from every unloving word, either to a present or of an absent person; in all his conversation aiming at this, either to improve himself in knowledge or virtue, or to make those with whom he converses some way wiser, or better, or happier than they were before.

9. The same love is productive of all right actions. It leads him into an earnest and steady discharge of all social offices, of whatever is due to relations of every kind: to his friends, to his country and to any particular community whereof he is a member. It prevents his willingly hurting or grieving any man. It guides him into a uniform practice of justice and mercy, equally extensive with the principle whence it flows. It constrains him to do all possible good, of every possible kind, to all men; and makes him invariably resolved in every circumstance of life to do that, and that only, to others, which supposing he were himself in the same situation, he would desire they should do to him.

10. And as he is easy to others, so he is easy in himself. He is free from the painful swellings of pride, from the flames of anger, from

the impetuous gusts of irregular self-will. He is no longer tortured with envy or malice, or with unreasonable and hurtful desire. He is no more enslaved to the pleasures of sense, but has the full power both over his mind and body, in a continued cheerful course of sobriety, of temperance and chastity. He knows how to use all things in their place and yet is superior to them all. He stands above those low pleasures of imagination which captivate vulgar minds, whether arising from what mortals term greatness, or novelty or beauty. All these too he can taste and still look upward, still aspire to nobler enjoyments. Neither is he a slave to fame; popular breath affects not him; he stands steady and collected in himself.

11. And he who seeks no praise cannot fear dispraise. Censure gives him no uneasiness, being conscious to himself that he would not willingly offend and that he has the approbation of the Lord of all. He cannot fear want, knowing in whose hand is the earth and the fullness thereof and that it is impossible for him to withhold from one that fears him any manner of thing that is good. He cannot fear pain, knowing it will never be sent unless it be for his real advantage, and that then his strength will be proportioned to it, as it has always been in times past. He cannot fear death, being able to trust him he loves with his soul as well as his body, yes, glad to leave the corruptible body in the dust, 'till it is raised, incorruptible and immortal. So that, in honour or shame, in abundance or want, in ease or pain, in life or death, always and in all things, he has learned to be content, to be easy, thankful, joyful, happy.

12. He is happy in knowing there is a God – an intelligent Cause and Lord of all – and that he is not the produce either of blind chance or inexorable necessity. He is happy in the full assurance he has that this Creator and End of all things is a being of boundless wisdom, of infinite power to execute all the designs of his wisdom and of no less infinite goodness to direct all his power to the advantage of all his creatures. Nay, even the consideration of his immutable justice, rendering to all their due, of his unspotted holiness, of his all-sufficiency in himself, and of that immense ocean of all perfections which

centre in God from eternity to eternity, is a continual addition to the happiness of a Christian.

13. A further addition is made thereto while, in contemplating even the things that surround him, that thought strikes warmly upon his heart – these are your glorious works, Parent of Good! – while he takes knowledge of the invisible things of God, even his eternal power and wisdom in the things that are seen, the heavens, the earth, the fowls of the air, the lilies of the field. How much more, while, rejoicing in the constant care which he still takes of the work of his own hand, he breaks out in a transport of love and praise, *O Lord our Governor! How excellent is your Name in all the earth; you that have set your glory above the heavens!* – while he, as it were, sees the Lord sitting upon his throne and ruling all things well; while he observes the general providence of God co-extended with his whole creation and surveys all the effects of it in the heavens and earth, as a well-pleased spectator; while he sees the wisdom and goodness of his general government descending to every particular, so presiding over the whole universe as over a single person, so watching over every single person as if he were the whole universe – how does he exult when he reviews the various traces of the Almighty Goodness in what has befallen himself in the several circumstances and changes of his own life, all which he now sees have been allotted to him and dealt out in number, weight, and measure. With what triumph of soul, in surveying either the general or particular providence of God, does he observe every line pointing out an hereafter, every scene opening into eternity?

14. He is peculiarly and inexpressibly happy in the clearest and fullest conviction: 'This all-powerful, all-wise, all-gracious Being, this Governor of all, loves *me*. This lover of my soul is always with me, is never absent; no, not for a moment. And I love him: there is none in heaven but thee, none on earth that I desire beside thee! And he has given me to resemble himself; he has stamped his image on my heart. And I live unto him; I do only his will; I glorify him with my body and my spirit. And it will not be long before I shall die unto him, I shall die into the arms of God. And then

farewell sin and pain, then it only remains that I should live with him forever.'

15. This is the plain, naked portraiture of a Christian. But be not prejudiced against him for his name. Forgive his particularities of opinion and (what you think) superstitious modes of worship. These are circumstances but of small concern and do not enter into the essence of his character. Cover them with a veil of love and look at the substance: his tempers, his holiness, his happiness. Can calm reason conceive either a more amiable or a more desirable character?

Is it your own? Away with names! Away with opinions! I care not what you are called. I ask not (it does not deserve a thought) what opinion you are of, so you are conscious to yourself that you are the man whom I have been (however faintly) describing.

Do not you know you ought to be such? Is the Governor of the world well pleased that you are not?

Do you at least desire it? I would to God that desire may penetrate your inmost soul and that you may have no rest in your spirit 'till you are not only almost but altogether a Christian!

SECTION II

1. The second point to be considered is: what is real, genuine Christianity – whether we speak of it as a principle in the soul or as a scheme or system of doctrine?

Christianity, taken in the latter sense, is that system of doctrine which describes the character above recited, which promises it shall be mine (provided I will not rest till I attain) and which tells me how I may attain it.

2. First, it *describes* this character in all its parts, and that in the most lively and affecting manner. The main lines of this picture are beautifully drawn in many passages of the Old Testament. These are filled up in the New, retouched and finished with all the art of God.

The same we have in miniature more than once; particularly in the thirteenth chapter of the first Epistle to the Corinthians, and in that discourse which St Matthew records as delivered by our Lord at his entrance upon his public ministry.

3. Secondly, Christianity *promises* this character shall be mine if I will not rest till I attain it. This is promised both in the Old Testament and in the New. Indeed the New is, in effect, all a promise, seeing every description of the servants of God mentioned therein has the nature of a command, in consequence of those general injunctions: *Be you followers of me, as I am of Christ* (1 Corinthians 11:1); *Be you followers of them who through faith and patience inherit the promises* (Hebrews 6:12). And every command has the force of a promise, in virtue of those general promises: *A new heart will I give you, and I will put my Spirit within you, and cause you to walk in my statutes, and ye shall keep my judgements, and do them* (Ezekiel 36:26–27). *This is the covenant that I will make after those days, says the Lord; I will put my laws into their minds and write them in their hearts* (Hebrews 8:10). Accordingly, when it is said, *You shall love the Lord your God with all your heart, and with all your soul, and with all your mind* (Matthew 22:37), it is not only a direction what I shall do, but a promise of what God will do in me, exactly equivalent with what is written elsewhere: *The Lord your God will circumcise your heart, and the heart of your seed* (alluding to the custom then in use) *to love the Lord your God with all your heart, and with all your soul* (Deuteronomy 30:6).

4. This being observed, it will readily appear to every serious person who reads the New Testament with that care which the importance of the subject demands that every particular branch of the preceding character is manifestly promised therein, either explicitly, under the very form of a promise, or virtually, under that of a description or command.

5. Christianity tells me, in the third place, how I may attain the promise, namely, by faith.

But what is faith? Not an opinion, no more than it is a form of words; not any number of opinions put together, be they ever so true. A string of opinions is no more Christian faith than a string of beads is Christian holiness.

It is not an assent to any opinion, or any number of opinions. A man may assent to three or three-and-twenty creeds; he may assent to all the Old and New Testament (at least, as far as he understands them) and yet have no Christian faith at all.

6. The faith by which the promise is attained is represented by Christianity as a power wrought by the Almighty in an immortal spirit inhabiting a house of clay, to see through that veil into the world of spirits, into things invisible and eternal; a power to discern those things which with eyes of flesh and blood no man hath seen or can see, either by reason of their nature, which (though they surround us on every side) is not perceivable by those gross senses, or by reason of their distance, as being yet afar off in the bosom of eternity.

7. This is Christian faith in the general notion of it. In its more particular notion, it is a divine evidence or conviction wrought in my heart that God is reconciled to *me* through his Son, inseparably joined with a confidence in him as a gracious, reconciled Father, as for all things, so especially for all those good things which are invisible and eternal.

To believe (in the Christian sense) is, then, to walk in the light of eternity and to have a clear sight of, and confidence in, the Most High, reconciled to me through the Son of his love.

8. Now, how highly desirable is such a faith, were it only on its own account? For how little does the wisest of men know of anything more than he can see with his eyes? What clouds and darkness cover the whole scene of things invisible and eternal? What does he know even of himself as to his invisible part, what of his future manner of existence? How melancholy an account does the prying, learned philosopher (perhaps the wisest and best of all heathens), the great, the venerable Marcus Antoninus, give of these things? What was the result of all his serious researches, of his high and deep contemplations? 'Either dissipation (of the soul as well as the body) into the common, unthinking mass or reabsorption into the universal fire (the unintelligent source of all things) or some unknown manner of conscious existence, after the body sinks to rise no more.' One of

these three he supposed must succeed death; but which, he had no light to determine. Poor Antoninus – with all his wealth, his honour, his power, with all his wisdom and philosophy!

> What points of knowledge did he gain?
> That life is sacred all – and vain!
> Sacred how high, and vain how low?
> He could not tell – but died to know.

9. He died to know! And so must you, unless you are now a partaker of Christian faith. Oh, consider this! Nay, and consider, not only how little you know of the immensity of the things that are beyond sense and time, but how uncertainly do you know even that little! How faintly glimmering a light is that you have? Can you properly be said to *know* any of these things? Is that knowledge any more than bare conjecture? And the reason is plain. You have no senses suited to invisible or eternal objects. What *desiderata* then, especially to the rational, the reflecting part of mankind, are these: a more extensive knowledge of things invisible and eternal, a greater certainty in whatever knowledge of them we have, and, in order to both, faculties capable of discerning things invisible?

10. Is it not so? Let impartial reason speak. Does not every thinking man want a window, not so much in his neighbour's as in his own breast? He wants an opening there of whatever kind that might let in light from eternity. He is pained to be thus feeling after God so darkly, so uncertainly; to know so little of God and indeed so little of any beside material objects. He is concerned that he must see even that little, not directly, but in the dim, sullied glass of sense and, consequently, so imperfectly and obscurely that 'tis all a mere enigma still.

11. Now, these very *desiderata* faith supplies. It gives a more extensive knowledge of things invisible, showing what eye had not seen, nor ear heard, neither could it before enter into our heart to conceive. And all these it shows in the clearest light, with the fullest certainty and evidence, for it does not leave us to receive

our notices of them by mere reflection from the dull glass of sense, but resolves a thousand enigmas of the highest concern by giving faculties suited to things invisible. Oh, who would not wish for such a faith, were it only on these accounts? How much more, if by this I may receive the promise, I may attain all that holiness and happiness?

12. So Christianity tells me and so I find it. May every real Christian say, 'I now am assured that these things are so; I experienced them in my own breast. What Christianity (considered as a doctrine) promised is accomplished in my soul.' And Christianity, considered as an inward principle, is the completion of all those promises. It is holiness and happiness, the image of God impressed on a created spirit; a fountain of peace and love springing up into everlasting life.

SECTION III

1. And this I conceive to be the strongest evidence of the truth of Christianity. I do not undervalue traditional evidence. Let it have its place and its due honour. It is highly serviceable in its kind and in its degree. And yet I cannot set it on a level with this.

It is generally supposed that traditional evidence is weakened by length of time, as it must necessarily pass through so many hands in a continued succession of ages. But no length of time can possibly affect the strength of this internal evidence. It is equally strong, equally new, through the course of seventeen hundred years. It passes now, even as it has done from the beginning, directly from God into the believing soul. Do you suppose time will ever dry up this stream? Oh no! It shall never be cut off.

Labitur et labetur in omne volubilis aevum
(It flows and goes on flowing through all the circling years.)

2. Traditional evidence is of an extremely complicated nature, necessarily including so many and so various considerations that only men of strong and clear understanding can be sensible of its full

force. On the contrary, how plain and simple is this and how level to the lowest capacity. Is not this the sum: *one thing I know; I was blind, but now I see* – an argument so plain that a peasant, a woman, a child, may feel all its force.

3. The traditional evidence of Christianity stands, as it were, a great way off, and therefore, although it speaks loud and clear, yet makes a less lively impression. It gives us an account of what was transacted long ago, in far distant times as well as places; whereas the inward evidence is intimately present to all persons, at all times and in all places. It is near you, in your mouth, and in your heart, if you believe in the Lord Jesus Christ. *This*, then, *is the record*, this is the evidence, emphatically so called, *that God has given unto us eternal life and this life is in his Son.*

4. If, then, it were possible (which I conceive it is not) to shake the traditional evidence of Christianity, still he that has the internal evidence (and every true believer has the witness or evidence in himself) would stand firm and unshaken. Still he could say to those who were striking at the external evidence, 'Beat on the sack of Anaxagoras,' but you can no more hurt *my* evidence of Christianity than the tyrant could hurt the spirit of that wise man.

5. I have sometimes been almost inclined to believe that the wisdom of God has, in most later ages, permitted the external evidence of Christianity to be more or less clogged and encumbered for this very end, that men (of reflection especially) might not altogether rest there, but be constrained to look into themselves also and attend to the light shining in their hearts.

Nay, it seems (if it may be allowed for us to pry so far into the reasons of the divine dispensations) that, particularly in this age, God suffers all kind of objections to be raised against the traditional evidence of Christianity that men of understanding (though unwilling to give it up, yet, at the same time they defend this evidence) may not rest the whole strength of their cause thereon but seek a deeper and firmer support for it.

6. Without this, I cannot but doubt whether they can long maintain their cause; whether, if they do not obey the loud call of

God and lay far more stress than they have hitherto done on this internal evidence of Christianity, they will not, one after another, give up the external, and (in heart at least) go over to those whom they are now contending with; so that, in a century or two, the people of England will be fairly divided into real deists and real Christians. And I apprehend this would be no loss at all, but rather an advantage to the Christian cause. Nay, perhaps it would be the speediest, yea, the only effectual way of bringing all reasonable deists to be Christians.

7. May I be permitted to speak freely? May I, without offence, ask of you that are called Christians, what real loss would you sustain in giving up your present opinion that the Christian system is of God? Though you bear the name, you are not Christians now: you have neither Christian faith nor love. You have no divine evidence of things unseen, you have not entered *into the holiest by the blood of Jesus.* You do not love God with all your heart; neither do you love your neighbour as yourself. You are neither happy nor holy. You have not learned in every state therewith to be content; to rejoice evermore, even in want, pain, death, and in everything to give thanks. You are not holy in heart: superior to pride, to anger, to foolish desires. Neither are you holy in life; you do not walk as Christ also walked. Does not the main of your Christianity lie in your opinion, decked with a few outward observances? For as to morality, even honest heathen morality – oh, let me utter a melancholy truth! – many of those whom you style deists, there is reason to fear, have far more of it than you.

8. Go on, gentlemen, and prosper! Shame these nominal Christians out of that poor superstition which they call Christianity. Reason, rally, laugh them out of their dead, empty forms, void of spirit, of faith, of love. Convince them that such unmeaning pageantry – for such it manifestly is if there is nothing in the heart correspondent with the outward show – is absolutely unworthy, you need not say of God, but even of any man that is endued with common understanding. Show them that while they are endeavouring to please God thus, they are only beating the air. Know your

time; press on; push your victories 'till you have conquered all that know not God. And then he, whom neither they nor you know now, shall rise and gird himself with strength and go forth in his almighty love, and sweetly conquer you all together.

9. Oh, that the time were come! How do I long for you to be partakers of the exceeding great and precious promises! How am I pained when I hear any of you using those silly terms which the men of form have taught you: calling the mention of the only thing you want 'cant'; the deepest wisdom, the highest happiness, 'enthusiasm'! What ignorance is this? How extremely despicable would it make you in the eyes of any but a Christian? But he cannot despise you, who loves you as his own soul, who is ready to lay down his life for your sake.

10. Perhaps you will say, 'But this internal evidence of Christianity affects only those in whom the promise is fulfilled. It is no evidence to *me*.' There is truth in this objection. It does affect them chiefly, but it does not affect them only. It cannot, in the nature of things, be so strong an evidence to others as it is to them. And yet it may bring a degree of evidence. It may reflect some light on you also.

For, first, you see the beauty and loveliness of Christianity, when it is rightly understood, and you are sure there is nothing to be desired in comparison of it.

Secondly, you know the scripture promises this and says it is attained by faith, and by no other way.

Thirdly, you see clearly how desirable Christian faith is, even on account of its own intrinsic value.

Fourthly, you are a witness that the holiness and happiness above described can be attained no other way. The more you have laboured after virtue and happiness, the more convinced you are of this. Thus far, then, you need not lean upon other men; thus far you have personal experience.

Fifthly, what reasonable assurance can you have of things whereof you have not personal experience? Suppose the question were, can the blind be restored to sight? This you have not yourself experienced. How then will you know that such a thing ever was? Can there be an easier or surer way than to talk with one or some number of men who were blind but are now restored to sight? They cannot be deceived as to the fact in question; the nature of the thing leaves no room for this. And if they are honest men (which you may learn from other circumstances), they will not deceive you.

Now transfer this to the case before us. And those who were blind, but now see – those who were sick many years, but now are healed; those who were miserable, but now are happy – will afford *you* also a very strong evidence of the truth of Christianity; as strong as can be in the nature of things 'till you experience it in your own soul. And this, though it be allowed they are but plain men, and, in general, of weak understanding; nay, though some of them should be mistaken in other points and hold opinions which cannot be defended.

11. All this may be allowed concerning the primitive Fathers. I mean particularly Clemens Romanus, Ignatius, Polycarp, Justin Martyr, Irenaeus, Origen, Clemens Alexandrinus, Cyprian; to whom I would add Macarius and Ephraim Syrus.

I allow that some of these had not strong natural sense, that few of them had much learning, and none the assistances which our age enjoys in some respects above all that went before.

Hence I doubt not but whoever will be at the pains of reading over their writings for that poor end will find many mistakes, many weak suppositions, and many ill-drawn conclusions.

12. And yet I exceedingly reverence them, as well as their writings, and esteem them very highly in love. I reverence them, because they were Christians, such Christians as are above described. And I reverence their writings, because they describe true, genuine Christianity, and direct us to the strongest evidence of the Christian doctrine.

Indeed, in addressing the heathens of those times, they intermix other arguments – particularly, that drawn from the numerous miracles which were then performed in the Church, which they needed only to open their eyes and see daily wrought in the face of the sun.

But still they never relinquish this: 'What the scripture promises, I enjoy. Come and see what Christianity has done here; and acknowledge it is of God.'

I reverence these ancient Christians (with all their failings) the more, because I see so few Christians now; because I read so little in the writings of later times, and hear so little, of genuine Christianity; and because most of the modern Christians (so called), not content with being wholly ignorant of it, are deeply prejudiced against it, calling it 'enthusiasm', and I know not what.

That the God of power and love may make both them, and you, and me, such Christians as those Fathers were, is the earnest prayer of, Reverend Sir,

Your real friend and servant,

John Wesley

1753

V

Covenant Service

1

Get these three principles fixed in your hearts: that things eternal are much more considerable than things temporal; that things not seen are as certain as the things that are seen; that upon your present choice depends your eternal lot. Choose Christ and his ways, and you are blessed forever; refuse, and you are undone forever. And then,

2 Make your choice

Turn either to the right hand or to the left; lay both parts before you, with every link of each; Christ with his yoke, his cross and his crown; or the Devil with his wealth, his pleasure and curse: and then put yourselves to it thus; soul, you see what is before you, what will you do? Which will you, either the crown or the curse? If you choose the crown, remember that the day you take this, you must be content to submit to the cross and yoke, the service and the sufferings of Christ, which are linked to it. What say you? Had you rather take the gains and pleasures of sin, and venture on the curse? Or will you yield yourself a servant to Christ, and so make sure the crown?

If your hearts fly off, and would fain waive the business, leave them not so. If you be unresolved, you are resolved; if you remain undetermined for Christ, you are determined for the Devil. Therefore give not off, but follow your hearts from day to day, let them not rest, till the matter be brought to an issue, and see that you make a good choice. This is your choosing the good part, God and the blessings of the world to come, for your portion and happiness; and in this is included your renouncing the world, and worldly happiness.

3 Embark with Christ

Adventure yourselves with him, cast yourselves upon his righteousness, as that which shall bring you to God; as a poor captive exile that is cast upon a strange land, a land of robbers and murderers, where he is ready to perish, and having no hope either of abiding there, or escaping home with life and meeting at length with a pilot that offers to transport him safely home, he embarks with him, and ventures himself, and all he has in his vessel – do you likewise: you are exiles from the presence of God, and fallen into a land of robbers and murderers; your sins are robbers, your pleasures are robbers, your companions in sin are robbers and thieves. If you stay where you are, you perish, and escape home of yourselves you cannot; Christ offers, if you will venture with him, he will bring you home, and he will bring you to God – Will you say now to him, *Lord Jesus, will you undertake for me? Will you bring me to God, bring me into the Land of Promise? With you I will venture myself; I cast myself upon you, upon your blood, upon your righteousness; I lay up all my hopes, and venture my whole interest, soul and body with you.*

This is closing with Christ as your Priest. And in this is included your renouncing your own righteousness; you can never, you will never cast yourselves on him alone, till all your hopes in yourselves have given up the ghost.

There are two things which must necessarily be supposed, in order to a sinner's coming to Christ: 1. *A deep sense of his sin and misery.* 2. *An utter despair of himself, and of all things else beside Christ.*

1. *A deep sense of his sin and misery.* No man will regard a Saviour, that doth not see himself a sinner; the whole regard not the physician. Therefore it is said that the Spirit of God, when he should come to christianize the world, should in the first place, *convince the world of sin* (John 16:8). He shall convince the world of sin; he shall demonstrate them sinners, bring up their sins before their eyes, bring home their sins upon their consciences, and make them see themselves, and feel themselves the most vile and abominable of creatures; sin

hides itself from the sinner's eyes, and all its vileness and deformity. But the Spirit of God plucks off the mantle, and makes sin appear to be sin; makes all the sinner's gods appear to be so many devils; brings forth the blackness and filthiness of sin into sight, makes the sinner see himself an unclean and abominable thing; and withal, he brings forth the guilt of sin, sets all these devils tormenting the sinner, filling him with fear, and terror, and amazement; in this respect he is called the spirit of bondage, that works fear and trouble in the heart; the Spirit's awakening a sleepy sinner is a kind of wakening in hell. *Lord what am I? What mean these legions round about me? These chains and fetters that are upon me? What means this black roll before my eyes, of curses, and wrath, and woes? Lord, where am I? Have I been playing, and sporting, and making merry, and my soul in such a case as this? But is there no hope of escaping out of this wretched state? I see there is no abiding thus, I am but a dead man, if I continue as I am. What may I do to be saved?*

When he is brought to this, there is some way made for his entertainment of Jesus; yet this is not all that is needful, but he must further be brought to:

2. *An utter despair of himself, and of all things else beside Christ.* Being made sensible of his sin, and of his danger, a sinner will look for help and deliverance; but he will look everywhere else, before he look unto Christ; nothing will bring a sinner to Christ but absolute necessity; he will try to forsake his sins, will think of leaving his drunkenness, and becoming sober; of leaving his adulteries, and becoming chaste, and so see if by this means he may not escape. He will go to prayers and sermons, and sacraments, and search out if there be no salvation in them; but all these, though they be useful in their places, yet looking no further, the sinner sees there is no help in them; his righteousness cannot help him, this is but rags; his duties cannot help him, these may be reckoned among his sins; ordinances cannot help, these are but empty cisterns; and all tell him, *You knock at a wrong door; salvation is not in us. Well, the Lord be merciful to me, says the sinner, what shall I do? Abide as I am, I dare not, and how to help*

myself I know not; my praying will not help me; if I give all my goods to the poor, if I should give my body to be burned, all this would not save my soul; woe is me, what shall I do, and whither shall I go?

And now, being brought to this distress, to this utter loss, his despair drives him to the only source of hope that is left open. Then Christ will be acceptable, when he sees none but Christ can help him, the Apostle tells us (Galatians 3:23), *We are kept under the Law, shut up unto the Faith, that should afterwards be revealed*: all other doors were shut up against us, there was no hope of escaping, but by that one door that was left open, *the faith that was afterwards to be revealed.* As the besieged in a city, that have every gate blocked up, and but one difficult passage left open, by which there is any possibility of escaping, thither throng for the saving of their lives; they are shut up unto that door, to which (if there had been any other way open) they would never have come.

And as Christ will never be accepted, so can the sinner never be received of him, till he lets go all other props, and trusts on him alone. Christ will have no sharer with him in the work of saving souls. *If you seek me, let these go their way,* as he said in another case; let not only your sins go, but let your righteousness go, all the refuge of lies wherein you have trusted; let all go, if you will have me to be a refuge to you. I came not to call the righteous; if I should, they would not come; or if they come, let them go as they came, let them go to their righteousness in which they trust, and let naked, destitute sinners, distressed sinners, come to me, who am come to this end, to seek and to save them that are lost.

Sinners, will you come now? Will you venture here? For this your adventuring on Christ, you have this threefold warrant:

(a) God's ordination. This is he, whom God the Father has appointed, and sent into the world, to bring back his exiles to himself, to save sinners. This is he whom God the Father has sealed, has marked him out for that chosen person, in whom is salvation; has sealed him his commission, for the redeeming and reconciling the world to himself. As God said unto the three friends of Job, when he was angry with them (Job 42:8), *Go to my servant Job, and he shall offer sacrifice for you, he shall pray for you, for him will I accept*: so to sinners, go, says the Lord, to my servant *Jesus*, he shall offer sacrifice for you, he shall make reconciliation for you (Isaiah 42:1), *Behold my Servant whom I uphold, my Elect in whom my soul delights: I have put my Spirit upon him, he shall bring forth judgement to the Gentiles.*

(b) God's command (1 John 3:23), *This is his commandment, that we should believe on the name of his Son Jesus Christ.*

(c) The promise of God (1 Peter 2:6), *Behold, I lay in Sion a chief cornerstone, elect, precious: he that believes on him shall not be confounded.*

Now having this threefold warrant, the warrant of God's *ordination, command,* and *promise,* you may be bold to adventure on Christ, and to apply yourselves to him thus: Lord Jesus, here I am, a poor captive exile, a lost creature, an enemy to God, under his wrath and curse; will you, Lord, undertake for me, reconcile me to God, and save my soul? Do not, Lord, refuse me, for if you refuse me, to whom then shall I go? Are you not he, and he alone, whom God the Father has sealed, the Saviour of sinners? The Lord God has sent me to you, has bid me come, he has commanded me to believe, and cast myself upon you. Lord Jesus, will you refuse to help a distressed creature, whom the Father has sent to you for your help? If I had come on my own head, or in my own name, you might well have put me back; but since I come at the command of the Father, reject me not; Lord, help me; Lord, save me. Are you not he concerning whom the Father has promised, *He that believes on him shall not be confounded*? I come, Lord; I believe, Lord; I throw myself upon your grace and mercy; I cast myself upon your blood and bowels, do not refuse me. I have nowhere else to go; here I will stay, I will not stir from your door; on you I will trust, and rest, and venture myself; God has laid my help on you, and on you I lay my hope for pardon, for life, for salvation; if I perish, I perish on your shoulders; if I sink, I sink in your vessel; if I die, I die at your door; bid me not go away, for I will not go.

4 Resign and deliver up yourselves to God in Christ

Yield *yourselves to the* Lord, that is, as his servants, give up the dominion and government of yourselves to Christ. *Neither yield your members, as instruments of unrighteousness unto sin, but yield yourselves to God, as those that are alive from the dead, and your members, as instruments of righteousness unto God. To whom you yield yourselves servants to obey, his servants you are, to whom you obey.* Yield yourselves so to the Lord that you may henceforth be the Lord's; *I am yours,* says the Psalmist. Those that yield themselves to sin, and the world, their hearts say, sin, I am yours; world, I am yours; riches, I am yours; pleasures, I am yours. I am yours, says the Psalmist; devoted to your fear, dedicated to your service; I am yours, save me; give yourselves to Christ; sinners, be devoted to his fear.

And this giving yourselves to him must be such as supposes that you be heartily contented (1) *that he appoint you your work*; (2) *that he appoint you your station.*

1. *That he appoint you your work*; that he put you to whatsoever he pleaseth. Servants, as they must do their master's work, so they must be for any work their master has for them to do; they must not pick and choose, this I will do, and that I will not do; they must not say this is too hard, or this is too mean, or this may be well enough let alone; good servants, when they have chosen their master, will let their master choose their work, and will not dispute his will, but do it.

Christ has many services to be done, some are more easy and honourable, others more difficult and disgraceful; some are suitable to our inclinations and interests, others are contrary to both; in some we may please Christ and please ourselves, as when he requires us to feed and clothe ourselves, to provide things honest for our maintenance, yes, and there are some spiritual duties that are more pleasing than others – as to rejoice in the Lord, to be blessing and praising of God, to be feeding ourselves with the delights and comforts of Religion; these are the sweet works of a Christian. But then there are other works wherein we cannot please Christ but by denying ourselves, as giving and lending, bearing and forbearing, reproving men for their sins, withdrawing from their company, witnessing against wickedness, when it will cost us shame and reproach; sailing against the wind; parting with our ease, our liberties, and accommodations for the name of our Lord Jesus.

It is necessary, beloved, to sit down and consider what it will cost you to be the servants of Christ, and to take a thorough survey of the whole business of Christianity, and not engage hand over head, to you know not what.

First, see what it is that Christ expects, and then yield yourselves to his whole will; do not think of compounding, or making your own terms with Christ, that will never be allowed you.

Go to Christ, and tell him, Lord Jesus, if you will receive me into your house, if you will but own me as your servant, I will not stand upon terms; impose upon me what conditions you please, write down your own articles, command me what you will, put me to anything you see as good; let me come under your roof, let me be your servant, and spare not to command me; I will be no longer my own, but give up myself to your will in all things.

2. *That he shall appoint you your station and condition*; whether it be higher or lower, a prosperous or afflicted state, be content that Christ should both choose your work, and choose your condition; that he should have the command of you, and the disposal of you. Make me what you will, Lord, and set me where you will; let me be a vessel of silver or gold, or a vessel of wood or stone, so I be a vessel of honour; of whatsoever form or metal, whether higher or lower, finer or coarser, I am content; if I be not the head, or the eye, or the ear, one of the nobler and more honourable instruments you will employ, let me be the hand, or the foot, one of the most laborious, and lowest, and most contemptible of all the servants of my Lord. Let my dwelling be upon the dunghill, my portion in the wilderness, my name and lot among the hewers of wood, or drawers of water, among the doorkeepers of your house; anywhere, where I may be serviceable. I put myself wholly into your hands; put me to what you will, rank me with whom you will; put me to doing, put me to suffering, let me be employed for you, or laid aside for you, exalted for you, or trodden under foot for you; let me be full, let me be empty, let me

have all things, let me have nothing; I freely and heartily resign all to your pleasure and disposal.

This is closing with Christ, as your King and sovereign Lord; and in this is included your renouncing the Devil and his works, the flesh and its lusts; together with your consenting to all the laws and ordinances of Christ, and his providential government.

Beloved, such a close with Christ as you have here been exhorted to is that wherein the essence of Christianity lies; when you have chosen the incorruptible crown, that is, when you have chosen God to be your portion and happiness; when you have adventured, and laid up your whole interest, and all your hopes with Christ, casting yourself wholly upon the merits of his righteousness; when you have understandingly and heartily resigned and given up yourselves to him, resolving forever to be at his command, and at his disposal; then you are Christians indeed, and never till then. Christ will be the Saviour of none but his servants; he is the Author of eternal salvation to those that obey him; Christ will have no servants but by consent; his people are a willing people; and Christ will accept of no consent but in full to all that he requires; he will be all in all, or he will be nothing.

5 CONFIRM AND COMPLETE ALL THIS BY SOLEMN COVENANT

Give yourselves to the Lord as his servants, and bind yourselves to him as his covenant-servants.

Upon your entering into covenant with God, the covenant of God stands firm to you; God gives you leave, every man, to put in his own name into the covenant-grant; if it be not found there at last, it will be your own fault; if it be not there, there will be nothing found in the whole covenant belonging unto you; if it be there, all is yours; if you have come into the bond of the covenant, you shall have your share in the blessings of the covenant. Deuteronomy 26:17–18, *You have avouched the Lord this day to be your God, to walk in his ways, and to keep his statutes, and his commandments, and his judgements, to hearken to his voice. And the Lord has avouched you this day to be his peculiar people, as he has promised you.* Observe it, the same day that they avouched the Lord to be their God, the same day the Lord avouched them to be his peculiar people; the same day that they engage to keep the commandments of God, the same day the Lord engages to keep his promise with them.

There is a twofold covenanting with God – *in profession, in reality* – an entering our names, or an engaging our hearts. The former is done in baptism, by all that are baptized, who by receiving that seal of the covenant are visibly, or in profession entered into it; the latter is also twofold:

1. Virtual – which is done by all those that have sincerely made that closure with God in Christ; those that have chosen the Lord, embarked with Christ, resigned up, and given themselves to the Lord are all engaged persons, and have virtually covenanted with him.

2. Formal – which is our binding ourselves to the Lord by solemn vow or promise to stand to our choice. And this may be either only inward in the soul, or outward, and expressed either by words, lifting up of the hands, subscribing the hand, or the like; and that by how much the more express and solemn our covenanting with God is, by so much the more sensibly is it like to hold our hearts to him. Now that which I would persuade you to is this solemn and express covenanting with God. Providence has lately brought to my hand the advice of a dear friend and faithful labourer in the work of the Lord about this matter, together with an excellent form of words proposed for the help of weak Christians, and aptly accommodated to all the substantials of our baptismal covenant; which having found great acceptance with many, I do with zeal, for the establishing of souls in holiness and comfort, commend it to the use not only of young converts, but of the more grown Christians that have not experienced this or the like course. And in order to the putting this matter into practice, I shall first give you these few directions.

First, set apart some time, more than once, to be spent in secret before the Lord (a) in seeking earnestly his special assistance and gracious acceptance of you; (b) in considering distinctly all the conditions of the covenant, as they have been laid before you; and (c) in searching your hearts whether you either have already, or can now freely make such a closure with God in Christ, as you have been exhorted to. In special, consider what your sins are, and examine whether you can resolve to forgo them all. Consider what the laws of Christ are, how holy, strict, and spiritual, and whether you can upon deliberation make choice of them all (even those that most cross your interests and corrupt inclinations) as the rule of your whole life. Be sure you be clear in these matters, see that you do not lie unto God.

Secondly, compose your spirits into the most serious frame possible, suitable to a transaction of so high importance. Thirdly, lay hold on the covenant of God, and rely upon his promise of giving grace and strength, whereby you may be enabled to perform your promise. Trust not to your own strength, to the strength of your own resolutions, but take hold on his strength.

Fourthly, resolve to be faithful. Having engaged your hearts, opened your mouths, and subscribed with your hands to the Lord, resolve in his strength never to go back. Lastly, being thus prepared, on some convenient time set apart for the purpose, set upon the work; and in the most solemn manner possible, as if the Lord were visibly present before your eyes, fall down on your knees, and spreading forth your hands toward heaven, open your hearts to the Lord, in these or the like words.

COVENANT PRAYER

O most dreadful God, for the passion of your Son, I beseech you to accept of your poor prodigal now prostrating himself at your door. I have fallen from you by my iniquity, and am by nature a son of death, and a thousandfold more the child of Hell by my wicked practice; but of your infinite grace you have promised mercy to me in Christ if I will but turn to you with all my heart. Therefore upon the call of your Gospel, I am now come in, and throwing down my weapons, submit myself to your mercy.

And because you require, as the condition of my peace with you, that I should put away my idols, and be at defiance with all your enemies, which I acknowledge I have wickedly sided with against you, I here from the bottom of my heart renounce them all; firmly covenanting with you, not to allow myself in any known sin, but conscientiously to use all the means that I know you have prescribed for the death and utter destruction of all my corruptions. And whereas I have formerly, inordinately and idolatrously let out my affections upon the world, I do here resign my heart to you that made it; humbly protesting before your glorious Majesty that it is the firm resolution of my heart, and that I do unfeignedly desire grace from you, that when you shall call me hereunto, I may practise this my resolution, to forsake all that is dear to me in this world, rather than turn from you, to the ways of sin; and that I will watch against all temptations, whether of prosperity or adversity, lest they withdraw my heart from you; beseeching you also to help me against the temptations of Satan, to whose wicked suggestions I resolve, by your grace, never to yield. And because my own righteousness is but menstruous rags, I renounce all confidence therein, and acknowledge that I am of myself a hopeless, helpless, undone creature, without righteousness or strength.

And forasmuch as you have, of your bottomless mercy, offered most graciously to me, wretched sinner, to be again my God through Christ, if I would accept of you; I call heaven and earth to record this day that I do here solemnly avouch you for the Lord my God; and with all veneration bowing the neck of my soul under the feet of your most sacred Majesty, I do here take you the Lord Jehovah, Father, Son, and Holy Ghost, for my portion; and do give up myself, body and soul, for your servant; promising and vowing to serve you in holiness and righteousness, all the days of my life. And since you have appointed the Lord Jesus Christ the only means of coming unto you I do here upon the bended knees of my soul accept of him as the only new and living way, by which sinners may have access to you; and do solemnly join myself in a marriage-covenant to him.

O blessed Jesus, I come to you hungry, wretched, miserable, blind, and naked; a most loathsome, polluted wretch, a guilty, condemned malefactor, unworthy to wash the feet of the servants of my Lord, much more to be solemnly married to the King of Glory; but since such is your unparalleled love, I do here with all my power accept you, and take you for my head and husband, for better, for worse, for richer, for poorer, for all times and conditions, to love, honour, and obey you before all others, and this to the death. I embrace you in all your offices; I renounce my own worthiness, and do here avow you for the Lord my Righteousness; I renounce my own wisdom, and do here take you for my only guide; I renounce my own will, and take your will for my law.

And since you have told me I must suffer if I will reign, I do here covenant with you to take my lot, as it falls, with you, and by your grace assisting to run all hazards with you, verily purposing that neither life nor death shall part between you and me.

And because you have been pleased to give me your holy laws as the rule of my life, and the way in which I should walk to your kingdom, I do here willingly put my neck under your yoke, and set my shoulder to your burden, and subscribing to all your laws as holy, just, and good, I solemnly take them as the rule of my words, thoughts, and actions; promising that though my flesh contradict and rebel, I will endeavour to order and govern my whole life according to your direction, and will not allow myself in the neglect of any thing that I know to be my duty.

Now, Almighty God, searcher of hearts, you know that I make this covenant with you this day, without any known guile or reservation, beseeching you, if you espy any flaw or falsehood therein, you would discover it to me, and help me to do it aright.

And now, glory be to you, O God the Father, whom I shall be bold from this day forward to look upon as my God and Father; that ever you should find out such a way for the recovery of undone sinners. Glory be to you, O God the Son, who have loved me, and washed me from my sins in your own blood, and are now become my Saviour and Redeemer. Glory be to you, O God the Holy Ghost, who by the finger of your almighty power have turned about my heart from sin to God.

O dreadful Jehovah, the Lord God Omnipotent, Father, Son, and Holy Ghost, you are now become my covenant-friend, and I, through your infinite grace, am become your covenant-servant. Amen. So be it. And the covenant which I have made on earth, let it be ratified in heaven.

FINAL RUBRIC

This covenant I advise you to make, not only in heart, but in word; not only in word, but in writing; and that you would with all possible reverence spread the writing before the Lord as if you would present it unto him as your act and deed: and when you have done this, set your hand to it: keep it as a memorial of the solemn transactions that have passed between God and you, that you may have recourse to it in doubts and temptations.

1780

Hymns of Charles Wesley: a Selection (1739–1762)

Servant of all, to toil for man

1 Servant of all, to toil for man
  Thou didst not, Lord, refuse;
Thy Majesty did not disdain
  To be employed for us!

2 Thy bright example I pursue,
  To thee in all things rise;
And all I think, or speak, or do,
  Is one great sacrifice.

3 Careless through outward cares I go,
  From all distraction free;
My hands are but engaged below –
  My heart is still with thee.

1739

Hark how all the welkin rings (Hark the herald angels sing)

1 Hark how all the welkin rings,
'Glory to the King of kings,
Peace on earth, and mercy mild,
God and sinners reconciled!'

2 Joyful, all ye nations, rise,
Join the triumph of the skies;
Universal Nature, say,
'Christ the Lord is born today!'

3 Christ, by highest heaven adored,
Christ, the everlasting Lord,
Late in time behold him come,
Offspring of a virgin's womb.

4 Veil'd in flesh, the Godhead see,
Hail the' Incarnate Deity!
Pleased as man with men to' appear
Jesus, our *Immanuel* here!

5 Hail the heavenly Prince of Peace!
Hail the Sun of Righteousness!
Light and life to all he brings,
Risen with healing in his wings.

6 Mild he lays his glory by,
Born – that man no more may die,
Born – to raise the sons of earth,
Born – to give them second birth.

7 Come, Desire of Nations, come
Fix in us thy humble home;
Rise, the woman's conquering Seed,
Bruise in us the serpent's head.

8 Now display thy saving power,
Ruin'd nature now restore;
Now in mystic union join
Thine to ours, and ours to thine.

9 *Adam's* likeness, Lord, efface
Stamp thy image in its place;
Second *Adam* from above,
Reinstate us in Thy love.

10 Let us thee, though lost, regain,
Thee, the Life, the Inner Man:
Oh! to all Thyself impart,
Form'd in each believing heart.

1739

Come, Holy Ghost, our hearts inspire

1 Come, Holy Ghost, our hearts inspire,
Let us thine influence prove,
Source of the old prophetic fire,
Fountain of life and love.

2 Come, Holy Ghost (for moved by thee
The prophets wrote and spoke);
Unlock the truth, thyself the key,
Unseal the sacred book.

3 Expand thy wings, celestial dove,
Brood o'er our nature's night;
On our disordered spirits move,
And let there now be light.

4 God through himself we then shall know,
If thou within us shine;
And sound, with all thy saints below,
The depths of love divine.

1740

Author of Faith, Eternal Word

1 Author of faith, eternal Word,
Whose spirit breathes the active flame,
Faith, like its finisher and Lord,
Today as yesterday the same;

2 To thee our humble hearts aspire,
And ask the gift unspeakable;
Increase in us the kindled fire,
In us the work of faith fulfil.

3 By faith we know thee strong to save
(Save us, a present Saviour thou!)
Whate'er we hope, by faith we have,
Future and past subsisting now.

4 To him that in thy name believes
Eternal life with thee is given;
Into himself he all receives –
Pardon, and holiness, and heaven.

5 The things unknown to feeble sense,
Unseen by reason's glimmering ray,
With strong commanding evidence
Their heavenly origin display.

6 Faith lends its realizing light,
The clouds disperse, the shadows fly;
Th' invisible appears in sight,
And God is seen by mortal eye.

1740

JESU, IF STILL THE SAME THOU ART

1 Jesu, if still the same thou art,
If all thy promises are sure,
Set up thy kingdom in my heart,
And make me rich, for I am poor:
To me be all thy treasures given,
The kingdom of an inward heaven.

2 Thou hast pronounced the mourners blest,
And lo! for thee I ever mourn.
I cannot, no, I will not rest
Till thou my only rest return;
Till thou, the Prince of peace, appear,
And I receive the Comforter.

3 Where is the blessedness bestowed
On all that hunger after thee?
I hunger now, I thirst for God!
See the poor fainting sinner, see,
And satisfy with endless peace,
And fill me with thy righteousness.

4 Ah, Lord! –if thou art in that sigh,
Then hear thyself within me pray.
Hear in my heart thy Spirit's cry,
Mark what my labouring soul would say,
Answer the deep, unuttered groan,
And show that thou and I are one.

5 Shine on thy work, disperse the gloom;
  Light in thy light I then shall see.
Say to my soul, 'Thy light is come,
  Glory divine is risen on thee;
Thy warfare's past, thy mourning's o'er;
Look up, for thou shalt weep no more.'

6 Lord, I believe the promise sure,
  And trust thou wilt not long delay;
Hungry, and sorrowful, and poor,
  Upon thy word myself I stay;
Into thine hands my all resign,
And wait till all thou art is mine!

1740

LET US JOIN ('TIS GOD COMMANDS)

1 Let us join ('tis God commands),
Let us join our hearts and hands;
Help to gain our calling's hope,
Build we each the other up.
God his blessing shall dispense,
God shall crown his ordinance,
Meet in his appointed ways,
Nourish us with social grace.

2 Let us then as brethren love,
Faithfully his gifts improve,
Carry on the earnest strife,
Walk in holiness of life.
Still forget the things behind,
Follow Christ in heart and mind;
Toward the mark unwearied press,
Seize the crown of righteousness!

3 Plead we thus for faith alone,
Faith which by our works is shown;
God it is who justifies,
Only faith the grace applies,
Active faith that lives within,
Conquers earth, and hell, and sin,
Sanctifies, and makes us whole,
Forms the Saviour in the soul.

4 Let us for this faith contend,
Sure salvation is its end;
Heaven already is begun,
Everlasting life is won.
Only let us persevere
Till we see our Lord appear;
Never from the rock remove,
Saved by faith which works by love.

1740

Jesus, the all-restoring Word

1 Jesus, the all-restoring Word,
My fallen spirit's hope,
After thy lovely likeness, Lord,
Ah, when shall I wake up?

2 Thou, O my God, thou only art
The Life, the Truth, the Way;
Quicken my soul, instruct my heart,
My sinking footsteps stay.

3 Of all thou hast in earth below,
In heaven above, to give,
Give me thy only love to know,
In thee to walk and live.

4 Fill me with all the life of love;
In mystic union join
Me to thyself, and let me prove
The fellowship divine.

5 Open the intercourse between
My longing soul and thee,
Never to be broke off again
To all eternity.

1740

JESU, LOVER OF MY SOUL

1 Jesu, Lover of my soul,
  Let me to thy bosom fly,
While the nearer waters roll,
  While the tempest still is high:
Hide me, O my Saviour, hide,
  Till the storm of life be past!
Safe into the haven guide,
  Oh, receive my soul at last!

2 Other refuge have I none,
  Hangs my helpless soul on thee;
Leave, ah! leave me not alone,
  Still support and comfort me:
All my trust on thee is stayed,
  All my help from thee I bring;
Cover my defenceless head
  With the shadow of thy wing.

3 Thou, O Christ, art all I want
  More than all in thee I find!
Raise the fallen, cheer the faint,
  Heal the sick, and lead the blind;
Just and holy is thy name,
  I am all unrighteousness;
False and full of sin I am,
  Thou art full of truth and grace.

4 Plenteous grace with thee is found,
  Grace to cover all my sin,
Let the healing streams abound;
  Make and keep me pure within:
Thou of life the fountain art,
  Freely let me take of thee,
Spring thou up within my heart,
  Rise to all eternity.

1740

LET EARTH AND HEAVEN AGREE

1 Let earth and heaven agree,
Angels and men be joined,
To celebrate with me
The Saviour of mankind;
T'adore the all-atoning Lamb,
And bless the sound of Jesu's name.

2 Jesus, transporting sound!
The joy of earth and heaven!
No other help is found,
No other name is given
By which we can salvation have:
But Jesus came the world to save.

3 Jesus, harmonious name!
It charms the hosts above;
They evermore proclaim,
And wonder at his love;
'Tis all their happiness to gaze,
'Tis heaven to see our Jesu's face.

4 His name the sinner hears,
And is from sin set free;
'Tis music in his ears,
'Tis life and victory;
New songs do now his lips employ,
And dances his glad heart for joy.

5 Stung by the scorpion sin
My poor expiring soul
The balmy sound drinks in,
And is at once made whole.
See there my Lord upon the tree!
I hear, I feel, he died for me.

6 O unexampled love!
O all-redeeming grace!
How swiftly didst thou move
To save a fallen race!
What shall I do to make it known
What thou for all mankind hast done!

7 Oh, for a trumpet-voice
On all the world to call,
To bid their hearts rejoice
In him who died for all!
For all my Lord was crucified,
For all, for all my Saviour died!

8 To serve thy blessed will,
Thy dying love to praise,
Thy counsel to fulfil,
And minister thy grace,
Freely what I receive to give,
The life of heaven on earth I live.

1742

Come, O thou Traveller unknown

1 Come, O thou Traveller unknown,
Whom still I hold, but cannot see!
My company before is gone,
And I am left alone with thee;
With thee all night I mean to stay,
And wrestle till the break of day.

2 I need not tell thee who I am,
My misery or sin declare;
Thyself hast called me by my name,
Look on thy hands, and read it there.
But who, I ask thee, who art thou?
Tell me thy name, and tell me now.

3 In vain thou strugglest to get free,
I never will unloose my hold;
Art thou the Man that died for me?
The secret of thy love unfold:
Wrestling, I will not let thee go
Till I thy name, thy nature know.

4 Wilt thou not yet to me reveal
Thy new, unutterable name?
Tell me, I still beseech thee, tell;
To know it now resolved I am:
Wrestling, I will not let thee go
Till I thy name, thy nature know.

5 What though my shrinking flesh complain
And murmur to contend so long?
I rise superior to my pain:
When I am weak, then I am strong;
And when my all of strength shall fail
I shall with the God-man prevail.

6 Yield to me now – for I am weak,
But confident in self-despair!
Speak to my heart, in blessings speak,
Be conquered by my instant prayer:
Speak, or thou never hence shalt move,
And tell me if thy name is *LOVE*.

7 'Tis Love! 'Tis Love! Thou diedst for me;
I hear thy whisper in my heart.
The morning breaks, the shadows flee,
Pure Universal Love thou art:
To me, to all, thy bowels move –
Thy nature, and thy name, is *LOVE*.

8 My prayer hath power with God; the grace
Unspeakable I now receive;
Through faith I see thee face to face;
I see thee face to face, and live!
In vain I have not wept and strove –
Thy nature, and thy name is *LOVE*.

9 I know thee, Saviour, who thou art –
Jesus, the feeble sinner's friend;
Nor wilt thou with the night depart,
But stay, and love me to the end:
Thy mercies never shall remove,
Thy nature, and thy name, is *LOVE*.

10 The Sun of Righteousness on me
    Hath rose with healing in his wings;
Withered my nature's strength; from thee
    My soul its life and succour brings;
My help is all laid up above:
Thy nature, and thy name, is *LOVE*.

11 Contented now upon my thigh
    I halt, till life's short journey end;
All helplessness, all weakness, I
    On thee alone for strength depend;
Nor have I power from thee to move:
Thy nature, and thy name, is *LOVE*.

12 Lame as I am, I take the prey,
    Hell, earth, and sin with ease o'ercome;
I leap for joy, pursue my way,
    And as a bounding hart fly home,
Through all eternity to prove,
Thy nature, and thy name, is *LOVE*.

1742

Oft I in my heart have said

1 Oft I in my heart have said,
Who shall ascend on high?
Mount to Christ my glorious head,
And bring him from the sky?
Borne on contemplation's wing,
Surely I should find him there,
Where the angels praise their King,
And gain the morning star.

2 Oft I in my heart have said,
Who to the deep shall stoop?
Sink with Christ among the dead,
From thence to bring him up?
Could I but my heart prepare,
By unfeigned humility,
Christ would quickly enter there,
And ever dwell with me.

3 But the righteousness of faith
Hath taught me better things:
'Inward turn thine eyes' (it saith,
While Christ to me it brings),
'Christ is ready to impart
Life to all for life who sigh;
In thy mouth, and in thy heart,
The word is ever nigh.'

1742

Come, thou long-expected Jesus

1 Come, thou long-expected Jesus,
Born to set thy people free,
From our fears and sins release us,
Let us find our rest in thee.
Israel's strength and consolation,
Hope of all the earth thou art;
Dear Desire of every nation,
Joy of every longing heart.

2 Born thy people to deliver,
Born a child and yet a king,
Born to reign in us forever,
Now thy gracious kingdom bring:
By thine own eternal Spirit
Rule in all our hearts alone;
By thine all-sufficient merit
Raise us to thy glorious throne.

1746

LOVE DIVINE, ALL LOVES EXCELLING

1 Love divine, all loves excelling,
Joy of heaven, to earth come down,
Fix in us thy humble dwelling,
All thy faithful mercies crown!
Jesu, thou art all compassion,
Pure, unbounded love thou art;
Visit us with thy salvation!
Enter every trembling heart.

2 Come, almighty to deliver,
Let us all thy grace receive;
Suddenly return, and never,
Never more thy temples leave.
Thee we would be always blessing,
Serve thee as thy hosts above,
Pray, and praise thee without ceasing,
Glory in thy perfect love.

3 Finish then thy new creation,
Pure and spotless let us be;
Let us see thy great salvation
Perfectly restored in thee;
Changed from glory into glory,
Till in heaven we take our place,
Till we cast our crowns before thee,
Lost in wonder, love, and praise.

1747

Happy the Man That Finds the Grace

1 Happy the man that finds the grace,
The blessing of God's chosen race,
The wisdom coming from above,
The faith that sweetly works by love.

2 Happy beyond description he
Who knows, the Saviour died for me,
The gift unspeakable obtains,
And heavenly understanding gains.

3 Wisdom divine! Who tells the price
Of wisdom's costly merchandise?
Wisdom to silver we prefer,
And gold is dross compared to her.

4 Her hands are filled with length of days,
True riches, and immortal praise;
Riches of Christ on all bestowed,
And honour, that descends from God.

5 To purest joys she all invites,
Chaste, holy, spiritual delights;
Her ways are ways of pleasantness,
And all her flowery paths are peace.

6 Happy the man who wisdom gains;
Thrice happy who his guest retains;
He owns, and shall forever own,
Wisdom, and Christ, and heaven are one.

1747

COME, SINNERS TO THE GOSPEL FEAST

1 Come, sinners to the gospel feast;
Let every soul be Jesu's guest;
Ye need not one be left behind,
For God hath bidden all mankind.

2 Sent by my Lord, on you I call;
The invitation is to all:
Come all the world; come, sinner, thou!
All things in Christ are ready now.

3 Come, all ye souls by sin oppressed,
Ye restless wanderers after rest;
Ye poor, and maimed, and halt, and blind,
In Christ a hearty welcome find.

4 Come, and partake the gospel feast,
Be saved from sin, in Jesus rest;
Oh, taste the goodness of your God,
And eat his flesh, and drink his blood.

5 Ye vagrant souls, on you I call
(Oh, that my voice could reach you all!):
Ye all are freely justified,
Ye all may live – for Christ hath died.

6 My message as from God receive:
Ye all may come to Christ, and live.
Oh, let his love your hearts constrain,
Nor suffer him to die in vain!

7 His love is mighty to compel;
His conqu'ring love consent to feel,
Yield to his love's resistless power,
And fight against your God no more.

8 See him set forth before your eyes,
That precious, bleeding sacrifice!
His offered benefits embrace,
And freely now be saved by grace!

9 This is the time: no more delay!
This is the acceptable day;
Come in, this moment, at his call,
And live for him who died for all!

1747

FORTH IN THY NAME, O LORD, I GO

1 Forth in thy name, O Lord, I go,
My daily labour to pursue,
Thee, only thee resolved to know
In all I think, or speak, or do.

2 The task thy wisdom has assigned
Oh, let me cheerfully fulfil,
In all my works thy presence find,
And prove thy acceptable will.

3 Thee may I set at my right hand
Whose eyes my inmost substance see,
And labour on at thy command,
And offer all my works to thee.

4 Give me to bear thy easy yoke,
And every moment watch and pray,
And still to things eternal look,
And hasten to thy glorious day;

5 For thee delightfully employ
Whate'er thy bounteous grace hath given,
And run my course with even joy,
And closely walk with thee to heaven.

1749

THEE, JESUS, FULL OF TRUTH AND GRACE

1 Thee, Jesus, full of truth and grace,
  Thee, Saviour, we adore;
Thee in affliction's furnace praise,
  And magnify thy power.

2 Thy power in human weakness shown
  Shall make us all entire;
We now thy guardian presence own,
  And walk unburnt in fire.

3 Thee, Son of man, by faith we see,
  And glory in our Guide,
Surrounded and upheld by thee,
  The fiery test abide.

4 The fire our graces shall refine
  Till, moulded from above,
We bear the character divine,
  The stamp of perfect love.

1749

COME ON, MY PARTNERS IN DISTRESS

1 Come on, my partners in distress,
My comrades through the wilderness,
Who still your bodies feel;
Awhile forget your griefs and fears,
And look beyond this vale of tears
To that celestial hill.

2 Beyond the bounds of time and space
Look forward to that heavenly place,
The saints' secure abode;
On faith's strong eagle pinions rise,
And force your passage to the skies,
And scale the mount of God.

3 Who suffer with our Master here,
We shall before his face appear,
And by his side sit down;
To patient faith the prize is sure,
And all that to the end endure
The cross, shall wear the crown.

4 Thrice blessed bliss-inspiring hope!
It lifts the fainting spirits up,
It brings to life the dead;
Our conflicts here shall soon be past,
And you and I ascend at last
Triumphant with our head.

5 That great mysterious Deity
We soon with open face shall see;
The beatific sight
Shall fill heaven's sounding courts with praise,
And wide diffuse the golden blaze
Of everlasting light.

6 The Father shining on his throne,
The glorious, co-eternal Son,
The Spirit, one and seven,
Conspire our rapture to complete,
And lo! we fall before his feet,
And silence heightens heaven.

7 In hope of that ecstatic pause,
Jesu, we now sustain the cross,
And at thy footstool fall,
Till thou our hidden life reveal,
Till thou our ravished spirits fill,
And God is all in all.

1749

JESUS, THOU SOUL OF ALL OUR JOYS

1 Jesus, thou soul of all our joys,
For whom we now lift up our voice,
And all our strength exert,
Vouchsafe the grace we humbly claim,
Compose into a thankful frame,
And tune thy people's heart.

2 While in the heavenly work we join,
Thy glory be our sole design,
Thy glory, not our own;
Still let us keep our end in view,
And still the pleasing task pursue,
To please our God alone.

3 The secret pride, the subtle sin,
Oh, let it never more steal in,
T'offend thy glorious eyes,
To desecrate our hallowed strain,
And make our solemn service vain,
And mar our sacrifice.

4 To magnify thy aweful name,
To spread the honours of the Lamb,
Let us our voices raise;
Our souls and bodies' powers unite,
Regardless of our own delight,
And dead to human praise.

5 Still let us on our guard be found,
And watch against the power of sound
With sacred jealousy;
Lest haply sense should damp our zeal,
And music's charms bewitch and steal
Our heart away from thee.

6 That hurrying strife far off remove,
That noisy burst of selfish love
Which swells the formal song;
The joy from out our heart arise,
And speak, and sparkle in our eyes,
And vibrate on our tongue.

7 Then let us praise our common Lord,
And sweetly join with one accord
Thy goodness to proclaim;
Jesus, thyself in us reveal,
And all our faculties shall feel
Thy harmonizing name.

8 With calmly reverential joy,
Oh, let us all our lives employ
In setting forth thy love;
And raise in death our triumph higher,
And sing, with all the heavenly choir,
That endless song above.

1749

My God, I am thine; what a comfort divine

1 My God, I am thine; what a comfort divine,
What a blessing to know that my Jesus is mine!
In the heavenly Lamb, thrice happy I am,
And my heart it doth dance at the sound of his name.

2 True pleasures abound in the rapturous sound;
And whoever hath found it hath paradise found.
My Jesus to know, and feel his blood flow,
'Tis life everlasting, 'tis heaven below!

3 Yet onward I haste to the heavenly feast;
That, that is the fullness, but this is the taste;
And this I shall prove, till with joy I remove
To the heaven of heavens in Jesus's love.

1749

THOU HIDDEN SOURCE OF CALM RESPOSE

1 Thou hidden source of calm repose,
Thou all-sufficient love divine,
My help and refuge from my foes,
Secure I am, if thou art mine:
And lo! from sin, and grief, and shame,
I hide me, Jesus, in thy name.

2 Thy mighty name salvation is,
And keeps my happy soul above;
Comfort it brings, and power, and peace,
And joy, and everlasting love:
To me with thy dear name are given
Pardon, and holiness, and heaven.

3 Jesu, my all in all thou art,
My rest in toil, my ease in pain;
The med'cine of my broken heart,
In war my peace, in loss my gain;
My smile beneath the tyrant's frown,
In shame my glory and my crown.

4 In want my plentiful supply,
In weakness my almighty power;
In bonds my perfect liberty,
My light in Satan's darkest hour;
In grief my joy unspeakable,
My life in death, my heaven in hell.

1749

SOLDIERS OF CHRIST, ARISE

1 Soldiers of Christ, arise,
And put your armour on,
Strong in the strength which God supplies
Through his eternal Son;
Strong in the Lord of hosts,
And in his mighty power,
Who in the strength of Jesus trusts
Is more than conqueror.

2 Stand then in his great might,
With all his strength endued,
But take to arm you for the fight
The panoply of God;
That having all things done,
And all your conflicts passed,
Ye may o'ercome through Christ alone
And stand entire at last.

3 Stand then against your foes
In close and firm array;
Legions of wily fiends oppose
Throughout the evil day;
But meet the sons of night,
But mock their vain design,
Armed in the arms of heavenly light,
Or righteousness divine.

4 Leave no unguarded place,
No weakness of the soul;
Take every virtue, every grace,
And fortify the whole;
Indissolubly joined,
To battle all proceed,
But arm yourselves with all the mind
That was in Christ your head.

1749

THOU, JESU, THOU MY BREAST INSPIRE

1 Thou, Jesu, thou my breast inspire,
And touch my lips with hallowed fire,
    And loose a stammering infant's tongue;
Prepare the vessel of thy grace,
Adorn me with the robes of praise,
    And mercy shall be all my song:
Mercy for all who know not God,
Mercy for all in Jesu's blood,
    Mercy, that earth and heaven transcends;
Love, that o'erwhelms the saints in light,
The length, and breadth, and depth, and height
    Of love divine, which never ends.

2 A faithful witness of thy grace,
Well may I fill th' allotted space,
    And answer all thy great design;
Walk in the works by thee prepared,
And find annexed the vast reward,
    The crown of righteousness divine.
When I have lived to thee alone,
Pronounce the welcome word, 'Well done!'
    And let me take my place above,
Enter into my Master's joy,
And all eternity employ
    In praise, and ecstasy, and love.

1749

Lo! He comes with clouds descending

1 Lo! He comes with clouds descending,
Once for favoured sinners slain;
Thousand thousand saints attending,
Swell the triumph of his train:
Hallelujah!
God appears on earth to reign.

2 Every eye shall now behold him
Robed in dreadful majesty;
Those who set at nought and sold him,
Pierced and nailed him to the tree,
Deeply wailing,
Shall the true Messiah see.

3 The dear tokens of his passion
Still his dazzling body bears;
Cause of endless exultation
To his ransomed worshippers;
With what rapture
Gaze we on those glorious scars!

4 Yea, Amen! let all adore thee,
High on thy eternal throne;
Saviour, take the power and glory
Claim the kingdom for thine own;
Jah, Jehovah,
Everlasting God, come down!

1758

O THOU WHO CAMEST FROM ABOVE

1 O thou who camest from above
    The pure celestial fire t'impart,
Kindle a flame of sacred love
    On the mean altar of my heart!

2 There let it for thy glory burn
    With inextinguishable blaze,
And trembling to its source return
    In humble love, and fervent praise.

3 Jesu, confirm my heart's desire
    To work, and speak, and think for thee;
Still let me guard the holy fire,
    And still stir up thy gift in me;

4 Ready for all thy perfect will,
    My acts of faith and love repeat,
Till death thy endless mercies seal
    And make the sacrifice complete.

1762

Index of Hymns

FOUNT CLASSICS

THE PILGRIM'S PROGRESS

John Bunyan

Written in prison, where Bunyan had been sent for unauthorized preaching, and first published in 1678, this classic story has been described as the most popular work of Christian spirituality written in English, and as the first English novel. It describes the road to the Celestial City, by way of Doubting Castle, the Delectable Mountains, Vanity Fair and other places whose names have entered the very fabric of the language.

Fascinating as literature, entertaining as story, profound as spiritual teaching for the soul's journey, *The Pilgrim's Progress* is 'a masterpiece which generation after generation of ordinary men and women have taken to their hearts'.

HUGH ROSS WILLIAMSON

FOUNT CLASSICS

POEMS AND DEVOTIONS

John Donne

John Donne was born in 1572 and, a Roman Catholic in his youth, took Anglican Orders in 1615 and was Dean of St Paul's from 1621 until his death.

His poetry, though forgotten for a long period, is the finest example of the so-called 'metaphysical' style – learned, allusive and witty. It is both highly physical and highly spiritual, with no distinction in method or content between the sacred and secular poems, both of which are included in this anthology.

Less well-known, but equally compelling, are his early *Devotions upon Emergent Occasions*, meditations and prayers issuing from a profound trust in God.

As Dean of St Paul's, Donne gained the reputation of being the finest preacher in the land; his use of strong rhythms and striking images made for powerful sermons. This volume contains edited versions of five of these, including the classic 'Death's Duel'.

FOUNT CLASSICS

TABLE TALK

Martin Luther

Translated by William Hazlitt

Martin Luther (1483–1546) was educated by the Augustian Hermits in Erfurt and at the University of Erfurt, becoming a professor in Wittenberg. He believed in the Pauline principle of justification by faith. This led him to challenge the corruption of the Roman Church – particularly the selling of indulgences – and to become the most famous leader of the Protestant Reformation.

Although Luther published a series of brilliant treatises in 1520, they make fairly heavy reading for the layperson. This volume is a selection of recollections, by friends and family, of things Luther said informally. As a result, it is an easily accessible and personal account of his feelings, ideas and even his humour.

Published here in its famous translation by William Hazlitt, the book celebrates the atmosphere of intellectual and spiritual freedom to be found in Germany at the beginning of the sixteenth century.

FOUNT CLASSICS

JOHN BUNYAN

The Christian

Gordon Wakefield

John Bunyan, born in 1628, son of a Bedford tinker and teenage soldier in the army of Robert Cromwell, fell into a kind of religious madness and emerged from this a soldier in the army of Christ: a fiery preacher in the radical Puritan tradition. His fervour brought him into conflict with the Restoration government, and he spent much time in prison. It was there he wrote his famous masterpiece, *The Pilgrim's Progress*. By the time of his death, he had written some 60 works.

This outstanding biography takes Bunyan seriously as a spiritual guide, and sets his life in the context of the history of English Christianity, as well as the political conflicts of his time.

'Wakefield's excellent book helps us to understand why Bunyan's influence continues down the centuries and across the continents.'

BAPTIST TIMES

'The chief merit of this impressive theological life is to bring back a Bunyan with a vibrant word for *now*, one that leaps all denominational frontiers.'

METHODIST RECORDER